DOCTOR TURNER'S
CASEBOOK

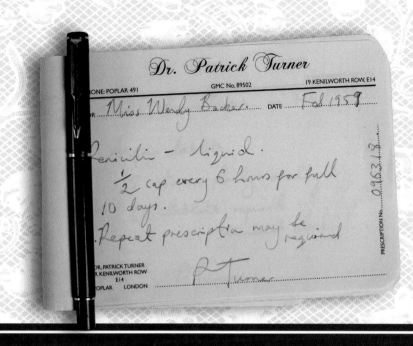

DOCTOR TURNER'S CASEBOOK

BASED ON THE BBC HIT DRAMA *CALL THE MIDWIFE*

STEPHEN McGANN

Introduction by HEIDI THOMAS

SIMON &
SCHUSTER

London · New York · Sydney · Toronto · New Delhi

A CBS COMPANY

First published in Great Britain by Simon & Schuster UK Ltd, 2016
A CBS company

Text written by Stephen McGann
Researcher: Karen Farrington
Set photographers: Series 1 & 2 Laurence Cendrowicz; Series 3 Laurence
Cendrowicz, John Rogers, Amanda Searle; Series 4 Laurence Cendrowicz,
Des Willie, Robert Viglasky; Series 5, medical kit and book cover, Sophie
Mutevelian

Publishing Director: Iain MacGregor
Designer: Ashley Western
Project Editor: Laura Nickoll
Editorial Assistant: Charlotte Coulthard

Call the Midwife
A Neal Street Production for the BBC

1 3 5 7 9 10 8 6 4 2

Simon & Schuster UK Ltd
1st Floor
222 Gray's Inn Road
London WC1X 8HB

www.simonandschuster.co.uk

Simon & Schuster Australia,
Sydney

Simon & Schuster India,
New Delhi

A CIP catalogue record for this book is available from the British Library

Hardback - 978-1-4711-5448-5
Ebook - 978-1-4711-5449-2

Printed and bound in Italy by L.E.G.O SpA

CONTENTS

Introduction   7

Childbirth: the Joy and the Jeopardy   16

Miracle Drugs   44

Losers in Poplar's Lottery of Life   56

Fragile Lives and Lost Hopes   76

The Shadow of Fear   100

Sheltering the Vulnerable   116

Outcasts: the Currency of Shame   146

The Legacy of War   168

The Vaccination Story   182

Britain Cleans Up   212

Timeline   244

Index   246

Picture credits   252

Acknowledgements   256

INTRODUCTION

As a drama series, *Call the Midwife* is set during a very particular time in British history, when society was shaking the dust of war from its shoes and turning to face a shining future. However, its themes of caring, healing and loving are timeless, with the work of its central characters recalling the philosophy of the ancient Greek doctor, Hippocrates: 'Treat often, cure sometimes, comfort always.'

Surrounded by the vibrant, committed women of Nonnatus House, Dr Turner began his *Call The Midwife* journey in a very small way, popping up only when his presence was absolutely necessary. In the opening series, his appearances were fleeting. We saw him arrive soon after the premature birth of Conchita Warren's twenty-fifth baby, late because of a call-out to a bronchial patient on a night of heavy smog. As the series progressed, we glimpsed him in the clinic, complimenting Chummy on her kindness to a sobbing, disabled mother – and later, stepping back to let her shine as she delivered a baby presenting in the breech position. In the final episode of Series One, he made a brief appearance in court in support of a rather ungrateful Sister Monica Joan when she was charged with shoplifting.

And that, in essence, was Dr Turner – harassed, humble, skilled and always kind. He was largely on the periphery of the major stories; standing by, hanging back, stepping in only when needed. This was not an especially accurate depiction of the busy and demanding life of an inner-city GP in the late fifties, but it did reflect the content of the bestselling *Call the Midwife* trilogy of novels by Jennifer Worth, on which the first and second television series were largely based.

Jennifer Worth herself had been deeply respectful of the doctors she knew in Poplar, once remarking that 'they really were terribly good at delivering babies'. But her memoirs were naturally centred on her own youthful career in midwifery, and when births went well (as most births do, when there are skilled midwives in attendance) there was seldom any need to send for the GP. 'Doctor' was only involved when there were complications.

Sadly, Jennifer Worth died of cancer just two weeks before we started filming the first series of *Call The Midwife*. During her final illness, I was blessed to spend some time with her. We talked at length about what the team might do to build on her rich legacy of stories and anecdotes, should the show continue for more than one season. We were both aware that the bulk of the stories in the trilogy had been used up in the first six episodes of the drama, and that Jennifer – who had faded fast after her diagnosis – would not be able to write any more. But she was well enough to talk through certain ideas I had already had, and to approve them. As part of this process, we also discussed which of the characters had been based on real people, and which had been wholly imaginary. There were quite a few names on the latter list, and among them were Dr Turner, who made only a handful of appearances in the books, and the similarly shadowy nun, Sister Bernadette.

Knowing that Dr Turner and Sister Bernadette had no real-life counterparts was exciting and rather liberating. Series One was successful enough to warrant an immediate re-commission, and Series Two would need to weave large amounts of new material around the remaining Jennifer Worth tales in order to create a satisfying whole. In terms of personal stories, I loved the idea of opening out all of the much-loved regular characters – offering up little titbits of back story, revealing secrets, giving each familiar face a past and somewhere to go. Dr Turner and Sister Bernadette were both wonderfully ripe for exploration.

However, *Call the Midwife* is a medical drama, not a soap opera, and the private lives of its characters will always be just a small part of a greater, more challenging whole. While writing Series Two, it became clear to me that the beating heart of *Call the Midwife* was not just the arrival of new life in the world, but the care and nurturing of life itself. It is a drama about the whole span of human experience – from the womb, through the cradle, to the grave. Trauma, sickness and suffering are an intrinsic part of that experience – and in Poplar, when help is needed, the Nonnatus House team, including Dr Turner, are there to provide it.

In addition, the late fifties and early sixties provided a rich seam of social and medical history that cried out to be mined and shared with our present-day, ten-and-a-half-million-strong audience. Therefore, as Series Two evolved into Series Three, Four and Five, and a sixth season was planned, *Call the Midwife* broadened its brief to include the district work of the Nonnatus House nurses on a regular basis. Stories of cystic fibrosis, tuberculosis and typhoid began to intertwine with tales of shoulder dystocia, post-partum haemorrhage and stillbirth. And Dr Turner was simply always there.

During the period in which *Call The Midwife* is set, general practitioners generally worked alone rather than in partnership with other doctors. Some, like Dr Turner, even set up and managed their own small maternity homes, working within financial parameters established by the NHS. However, their autonomy came at a price – urban GPs simply never stopped working. After morning surgery, the doctors made house calls, then attended community clinics in the afternoon, and after their subsequent evening surgery would be on call throughout the night.

What sort of a man (and in the fifties, most general practitioners were men) would choose to work so hard, and for a comparatively modest wage? As Dr Turner's character developed, the answer became obvious. A clever

Dr Patrick Turner (Stephen McGann)

man, a caring man; a man at once tireless and almost exhausted, determined to give the best he can to a community that needs him.

In the first Christmas Special, we learned that Dr Turner had lost his wife almost twelve months earlier, leaving him alone with his ten-year-old son, Timothy. His struggle to balance his job with single parenthood was summed up in a single scene, in which we saw him driving to visit the elderly Mrs Jenkins at home after she collapsed. Timothy was in the passenger seat of the car, eating chips out of newspaper in lieu of an evening meal – and when Dr Turner discovered the appalling conditions in which Mrs Jenkins was living, he simply went back to the car, took the chips off his child and handed them to his patient. Timothy, not unreasonably, was furious. However, the instinctive compassion of his father's gesture was exactly what the situation called for, fulfilling Mrs Jenkins' physical need for nourishment while working at gaining her trust.

Medicine, like nursing or the religious life, is a vocation in the purest sense – a calling. A practitioner of my own acquaintance once observed that 'you don't choose the career; the career chooses you', and I always sensed that Dr Turner had felt drawn to the healing profession from an early age. Born in Liverpool in 1909, his earliest memories would have been of wounded soldiers being wheeled through the city's parks in bath chairs, or limping on crutches, dressed in 'hospital blue' uniforms. Aged ten, he would have been acutely aware of the devastation wrought by the Spanish influenza epidemic, and the bus ride from his suburban home to his respected school, Liverpool Collegiate, would have taken him through some of the most deprived areas of the city.

When Dr Turner qualified, in the mid-thirties, he was determined to work with the urban poor, and spent the early years of his career in an impoverished hospital near the Liverpool docks. Working on the hectic Admissions ward, he became familiar with septicaemia, cancer, industrial accidents and the diseases that thrive where nutrition and sanitation are poor: diarrhoea, conjunctivitis, tuberculosis and rickets.

When World War Two broke out, Dr Turner – ever driven by the need to serve – volunteered for the Royal Army Medical Corps. Rising to the rank of major, he was initially posted to military hospitals in the British Isles, but later saw active service in the European theatre of war. In Italy, he commanded a tented field hospital, treating injured soldiers while under near-constant artillery and mortar bombardment. His courage and energy seemed limitless, but he was more vulnerable than he appeared. Towards the end of the war, Dr Turner suffered a nervous breakdown – described in his medical records as 'war neurosis' – and received in-patient treatment at a psychiatric hospital. For years afterwards, he nursed the shame of this in secret, telling no one. Until he finally confided in Shelagh some months after their marriage, the only reference ever made to it was an oblique one – his gentle, sensitive treatment of those whose own minds had fractured, and needed to be healed.

In the years immediately after the war, Dr Turner had three main reasons to live – his new and happy marriage to the former Marianne Parker, their baby son and the 1948 arrival of the National Health Service. Freshly established in London as a GP, he was energised, inspired and enthralled by the prospect of delivering free health care and medicine to every man, woman and child who required it. He was now fully engaged in fighting a new and supremely winnable war, in which the casualties were not human beings but suffering, pain and disease. He also had new and wonderful weapons in his armoury: penicillin, vaccination and previously unavailable diagnostic tools.

By the time *Call the Midwife* picks up Dr Turner's story, in the late fifties, he has been in Poplar for more than a decade, working closely with the sisters and nurses of Nonnatus House. The sight of his little green car outside a house or a block of flats is a familiar one, and a sign of significant happenings within. He might be bringing a child into the world with the aid of forceps, or administering morphine to ease an old man's final days. He might be longing for a cup of tea, dreaming of a sandwich, yearning for his bed. But he works on, because he is needed.

Stephen McGann, who plays Dr Turner, happens to be my husband. Very early on in the *Call The Midwife* process, when the character amounted to little more than a name, a leather bag and a few lines here and there, he came home from his first costume fitting and I asked how the character's 'look' was shaping up. He described to me how he had spent some time perusing the suits available at Angel's, the great film and television costumier. In the end, he had chosen one with a small darn in the knee – it spoke to him not just of Dr Turner's lack of concern with material things, but of his willingness to kneel at the bedside of his patients, wearing himself literally threadbare in their service.

Over the past few years, the thing said most often to me about Dr Turner is that he is the doctor everyone would like to have. In fact, he is the doctor many of us do have. He is highly trained, a good communicator, able to switch from an administrative to a counselling role at the drop of a hat, while also knowing how to hold a baby, or a dying person's hand. He is sometimes frustrated by red tape and regulations, and is as swift to berate the NHS in practice as he is to revere its unique and noble principles. But, like countless other brave and beleaguered general practitioners, Dr Turner gets up every day and does what he can to make the world a better place, tackling its challenges one patient at a time.

This book is dedicated to all general practitioners, past, present and future, in acknowledgement and appreciation of the service they give, have given and will give. Long may they 'comfort always'.

HEIDI THOMAS
SERIES CREATOR AND EXECUTIVE PRODUCER

THIS BOOK IS DEDICATED
TO ALL GENERAL PRACTITIONERS,
PAST, PRESENT AND FUTURE,
IN ACKNOWLEDGEMENT
AND APPRECIATION OF
THE SERVICE THEY GIVE,
HAVE GIVEN AND WILL
GIVE. LONG MAY THEY
'COMFORT ALWAYS'.

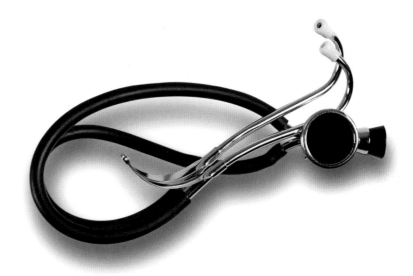

Dr. Patrick Turner

PHONE: POPLAR 491	GMC No. 89502	19 KENILWORTH ROW, E14

FOR .... DATE ....

CHAPTER 1

Childbirth: the Joy and the Jeopardy

19, KENILWORTH ROW
E14
POPLAR   LONDON ....

PRESCRIPTION No. ....

TWIN BIRTH

THE UNEXPECTED NEED NOT MEAN THE WORST. I write this lying in my bed, trying to steal an hour's sleep before surgery, after being up all night at an extremely difficult birth. Some hope.

I can remember Marianne stitching those curtains. That old machine of hers with the clattering wheel. I'd wanted something heavier to block the light, but fashion won the day. I'm glad. The light seeping through the pattern feels mischievous and warm. Like her victorious smile.

Mave Carter's birth was never going to be a normal affair - but an unexpected twin with transverse lie, right shoulder presentation and a forceps delivery wasn't what we'd bargained for. Not to mention the presence of Mave's sister Meg - whose unhelpful contribution even descended into physical abuse. Sister Bernadette showed remarkable patience considering the clout she'd taken. One of many admirable and surprising qualities she revealed.

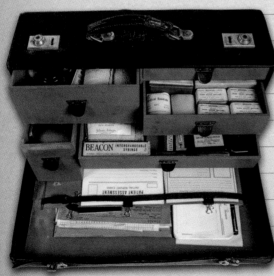

The idea that a twin can go to term undetected may seem surprising. Yet a second foetal heartbeat can elude the best of us, hidden behind a sibling in the womb. Mave Carter had been similarly hidden by her sister, and so evaded the clinical attention that might have

revealed the truth. Or perhaps not. Mother Nature can keep a secret longer than we think … the good and the bad.

On the day Marianne received her diagnosis, we'd been shopping for Tim's school uniform. The sun shone and the future seemed bright with ordinary cares. Much later, when the cancer took a hold, the pain would keep her awake till morning. I'd bring tea and draw the curtains against the day. She preferred the sunlight. I couldn't find it any more.

It was overcast when we buried her. Tim wore his uniform.

When Mave Carter finally delivered her second, the baby wasn't breathing. I presumed the worst. Yet Sister Bernadette took the child and performed Dr Eve's rocking method of artificial respiration on her. She believed that by rolling the infant's body back and forth headways, those tiny lungs might be encouraged to inflate. It seemed a vain hope, but she persisted - eyes never leaving the child. There was fire in her gentle determination. A preference for sunlight. The ghastly silence was broken by a lusty cry. Her skill and faith had charmed new life into the world.

The sun was shining when we left. The profound experience had lent the moment a pleasant informality. She surprised me again by sharing my cigarette - and even confessed to stealing her father's cigarettes as a child! Then, in a moment, she was gone, cycling back to the convent.

And here I am lying in my bed, the morning sunlight streaming through the closed curtains. The adrenalin is still racing.

THE UNEXPECTED NEED NOT MEAN THE WORST.

Diligent and devoted, Dr Turner is resolutely determined to extend the best-available medical care to those in his still-shabby side of London.

Even the most impoverished and marginalised in Poplar are entitled to help now the National Health Service is up and running. Dr Turner makes it his business to ensure that they are not forgotten, despite their meagre circumstances.

In searching for the right diagnosis he looks beyond the humble surroundings that anchor many of his patients to the bottom of the social pile. As well, he can see through the bravado that masks the fears of the neighbourhood's toiling men, and the wilful pride disguising the problems that regularly beset the women there.

If he encounters a baffling or obscure dilemma then he quests to find the solution, revealing the professionalism he has in common with thousands of other doctors of

Dr Turner has a broad brief, but it is caring for expectant mothers and newborns that he finds most rewarding.

the era. At times battling his own demons, he empathises with those wrestling theirs.

Dr Turner has a broad brief, but it is caring for expectant mothers and newborns that he finds most rewarding.

He's seen numerous changes since starting out as a doctor, when most births happened in a woman's bedroom no matter how shambolic that might be.

However, the case for home births suffered a number of setbacks in the fifties and sixties. Questions were being asked about the safety of having a baby in an ill-equipped bedroom when the alternative

Even after the Blitz Poplar was subject to air raids. This picture shows demolition squads moving into the High Street after a destructive attack in 1944.

Left: This machine, called a Blease pulmoflater and designed to administer Trilene, was manufactured as late as 1973, even though gas and air was by then the first choice of pain relief among most women.

Right: A gas and air machine c. late fifties, named after Lucy Baldwin (1869–1945), wife of the British Prime Minister Stanley Baldwin and campaigner for maternal health.

was a ward with all the latest medical equipment on hand. Moreover, pregnant women were not only concerned about the safety of their babies, but also what they would have to endure in labour.

There were already some forms of pain relief in use. Trilene was the anaesthetic form of a chemical called trichloroethylene, similar in smell to its close cousin used in dry-cleaning.

Trilene was less toxic than chloroform, another of the alternatives at the time. This nineteenth-century drug had an illustrious history in childbirth.

Queen Victoria had been given chloroform when she had her eighth child, Prince Leopold, in 1853. It was, she declared, 'delightful beyond measure' to produce a baby without the attendant agonies. It was still in use by the time of *Call the Midwife.*

Developed by Imperial Chemical Industries (ICI), Trilene was introduced as early as the forties for women in labour, although it was also used in dentistry and for minor surgery. It was administered through a face mask attached to a vaporising chamber by rubber tubing. Distinguished by its vivid blue colour, Trilene was far from universal, even at the end of the fifties. Although Trilene sets were more portable than the newly arrived gas and air equipment, 1957 figures show that there was only one set for every six community midwives nationwide.

GAS AND AIR

'BE CAREFUL WHAT YOU WISH FOR.' If this old adage existed in the form of a gas, then I'm certain it would possess the properties of nitrous oxide. I've recently acquired - at long last - a portable device for the delivery of pain relief to mothers in labour. Wonderful thing. It's far more effective than Trilene - providing a self-regulating mixture of nitrous oxide to the patient that eases the pain of contraction without hindering the process of birth. I've campaigned for this for some time.

Some of the sisters seem rather less thrilled. Maybe they feel it distracts mothers from the broader reality of their task, or encourages them to seek escape from what must be endured. On the contrary, I think it expresses the contribution our new Health Service can make to the lives of those in our care. An easing of distress, both immediate and long-term.

I had an opportunity last week to demonstrate the effectiveness of this apparatus when I was called to the labour of Mrs Collins - a rather spirited mother in my care. I'd explained the benefits of gas

I've recently acquired — at long last — a portable device for the delivery of pain relief to mothers in labour. Wonderful thing. It's far more effective than Trilene.

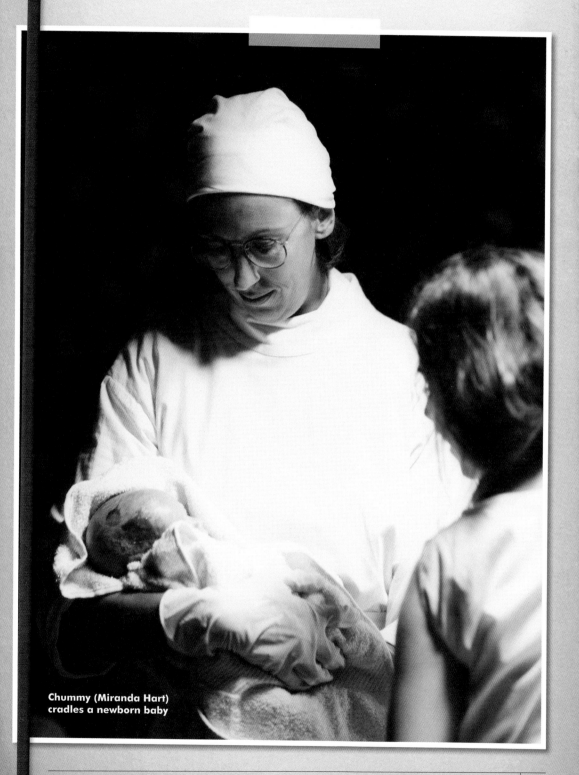

Chummy (Miranda Hart)
cradles a newborn baby

and air to her during a recent pre-natal clinic. I arrived to find her in advanced labour and calling for the pain relief I could provide. Her request brooked little argument, and could be heard by residents in the square below! Luckily I had the portable device in my car boot, and so was able to bring it upstairs for use at her bedside. The effect was immediate – a calm and healthy delivery. A grateful Mrs Collins suggested that word of my portable wonder might soon spread among the mothers of Poplar.

I was soon to marvel at Mrs Collins' capacity for understatement, while questioning the suitability of the word 'portable'.

My new device is portable only in the way a sack of coal is portable – while the mothers of Poplar tend to inhabit tenement apartments many floors high. Once word of Mrs Collins' birth was out, it seemed I was required at every high landing in the district. Unfortunately the midwives can't help, as the apparatus can't be carried by bicycle. I must haul these coals alone – a victim of my own success!

It's immensely rewarding to see the effect on the mothers in my care, who've been overlooked for too long with regard to this technology. Yet I've not been so exhausted since basic training – and I was considerably younger then. I'd be happy if I never saw another flight of tenement stairs. My poor feet!

Even Tim has taken pity on me, and suggested he might drive us to the fish and chip shop to spare my blisters. I explained that my subsequent arrest for allowing a minor to drive my car might involve rather more legwork.

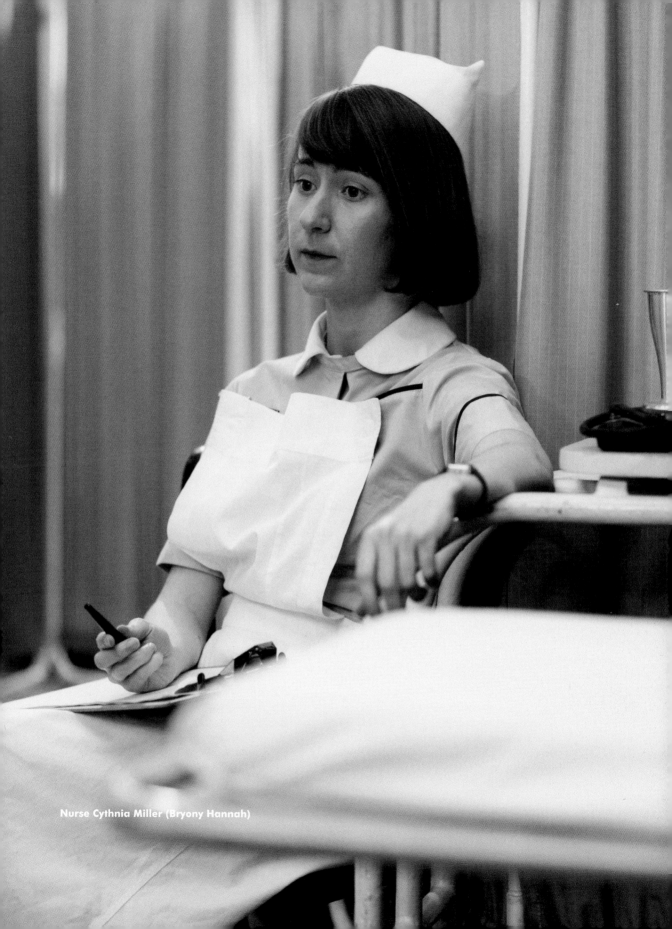

Nurse Cythnia Miller (Bryony Hannah)

The first woman in America to benefit from anaesthetic during labour was Fanny Longfellow, the wife of poet Henry Wadsworth Longfellow, who was given ether by her dentist in 1847. It had been difficult to persuade any medic to administer pain relief but, having heard about a British doctor helping a woman in childbirth in the same way, Fanny was determined. After delivering a healthy baby girl, her third child, she was thrilled by the pain-free labour.

Yet despite these high-profile fans of pain relief there was a cultural reluctance surrounding the issue, rooted firmly in the notion that God had made childbirth painful as a punishment to Eve after she tasted the apple in the Garden of Eden. Despite the advances in science and reason, Western society was still largely locked into tenets of faith. It wasn't until 1956 that Pope Pius XII pronounced on the issue, declaring that Christian women could be given pain relief, but warning that they shouldn't 'use it with exaggerated haste'.

There's also disturbing evidence that pain relief was withheld from unmarried mothers as a kind of arbitrary punishment for their predicament. One woman, who gave birth in 1961, has since recalled her stay in hospital, when she was told by another pregnant woman sharing the same ward that she was 'unsuitable' company.

In labour she was left alone as her contractions became more intense. 'I was lying on a hard table with one pillow but no covering at all. I was getting colder as the night moved on; I was wearing a gown with a gap down the back. I was informed that a woman like me couldn't expect to get any sympathetic treatment, and to stop making an unnecessary fuss. There was no pain relief for me – the gas and air machine had no face mask.' At that time gas and air was still the favoured option.

Pethidine was developed during the Second World War in Germany for the treatment of wounded soldiers. Initially it was sold over the counter for general aches and pains – and that resulted in the creation of 900 pethidine addicts. But from 1949 it was used during childbirth for pain relief, where its 'once only' application countered its addictive qualities. An opioid, it mimics the body's endorphins to block the sensation of contractions, sometimes causing side effects such as nausea and drowsiness.

The age of epidurals was just beginning, but got off to a slow start. As early as 1909, German obstetrician Walter Stoeckel (1871–1961) was administering the first caudal anaesthetics. However, the practice was not widely adopted.

In 1921 Spanish doctor Fidel Pages (1886–1923) experimented further with anaesthetic injections into the lumbar and thoracic regions. With improvements in needles, catheters and drugs, techniques were refined during the first half of the twentieth century. But although they were used occasionally in the fifties, they weren't commonly available during childbirth for another twenty years. Caesareans, meanwhile, were a rarity.

The most likely way to gain access to any of these drugs seemed to be by booking a hospital stay. At the time, though, there was a perpetual shortage of beds. In 1959 the Maternity Service

> While hospital admissions for childbirth were escalating, home births remained the hallmark of poorer neighbourhoods such as Poplar.

A woman demonstrates a portable gas and air machine known as 'Queen Charlotte's Gas Air Analgesia Apparatus' as early as 1937. Although bulky, it was intended for use at home births and could also be taken to the site of industrial accidents.

Committee recommended that there should be sufficient hospital beds for 70 per cent of all deliveries, a somewhat arbitrary figure derived from outmoded data. But this would be enough to cater for all emergencies, older first-time mothers, those expected to have difficulties in labour and the growing number who chose to have their babies in hospital.

However, demand soon outstripped supply. On 29 October 1959 Parliament heard from Manchester MP Eric Johnson about the shortage of beds for mothers-to-be in his constituency. After being told that no bed would be available in hospital when they came to give birth, women went away 'in tears, feeling bitterly resentful'.

According to his figures, fewer than 60 per cent of Manchester women gave birth in hospital in 1957, compared with more than 80 per cent in London, while the figure for both Leeds and Liverpool was 68.7 per cent. With its 345 hospital beds fully subscribed, Manchester doctors sometimes had to compromise on the ten-day recommended lying-in period, he claimed. (At the time a ten-day stay in hospital was the norm, but a discussion about the length needed for 'lying-in' was beginning, and a 48-hour period was being mooted as acceptable as long as the doctor and local authority had been consulted in advance and the home circumstances were considered 'satisfactory'.)

While hospital admissions for childbirth were escalating, home births remained the hallmark of poorer neighbourhoods such as Poplar. Afterwards GPs like Dr Turner would have cuddled the new arrival and tended to the mother. These were times of heightened emotions, when the doctor had worked wordlessly in harmony with midwives like Sister Bernadette, with a shared goal that far exceeded mere job satisfaction. The bonds developed in such a rarified atmosphere ran deep.

Imagine the shock, then, for him as much as everyone else when either baby or mother died.

COT DEATH

NOTHING CAN PREPARE YOU FOR THE SUDDEN DEATH OF AN INFANT. No amount of clinical experience or years in the surgery. Such an event calls for answers that the moment itself can never fully provide.

I was called to the house of Patrick and Rene Kelly to attend their newborn son. When I arrived, it was clear the infant was dead. The cold discoloration in a face so recently alive never fails to steal the breath. I performed my examination in a room filled with desperate hope and a rising horror. At such a moment a doctor must answer emotion with truth, and their own disquiet with a dedication to procedure. It's a difficult task.

Young Nurse Miller was in attendance - and I could see the experience had been difficult for her. I trust Nonnatus House to provide good support at times like this. Sudden death requires a post-mortem, and so a private tragedy can soon become a very public one for those involved.

The Kelly family are devoutly religious, and their loss required a context I felt unable to provide. I have no faith myself, yet I'm sincerely moved by its power to move others. Sister Julienne was present and so was able to lead the family in an affecting prayer for the life they'd lost. A medic would be a fool not to recognise the therapeutic strength in such a moment.

A doctor must trust in a different form of kindness. Our task is to dignify loss with facts. By finding the true cause of little Thomas's

death, we can provide a way for those involved to move on from the shock of events. In the places where faith has only questions, our answers can be a stepping-stone to healing.

A small exchange this evening made me consider these matters afresh. I had called by Nonnatus House to review Nurse Miller's notes on the Kelly birth, hoping for some insight into the infant's death in advance of the inquiry. Sister Bernadette, a young nun of the order, brought me tea. I remarked to her that at these difficult times, I wished I possessed her faith. I was surprised to hear the sister respond that she doubted her faith made any difference. I've wondered at her meaning ever since. Perhaps our mistake is to think that faith and fact are separate paths to human consolation. Perhaps neither can provide adequate responses to the enormity of life's losses without the presence of the other.

Patrick and Rene Kelly deserve all the consolation that life can provide - and from all the sources that can provide it. Sister Bernadette's humility in the face of this burden humbles me. Not all things may be known - but all might still be given.

> *Perhaps our mistake is to think that faith and fact are separate paths to human consolation. Perhaps neither can provide adequate responses to the enormity of life's losses without the presence of the other.*

Sudden infant death syndrome (SIDS) is the unexpected and inexplicable death of an apparently healthy infant, usually during sleep. More commonly known as cot death, it is inevitably the trigger for a tidal wave of grief among parents, siblings and the wider family. During the era of *Call the Midwife*, little was known about what prompted cot deaths, which most commonly occur in babies aged between two and four months. However, for the first time, in the fifties the fate of infants was becoming a cause for public concern.

Previously families had tended to mushroom with numerous children, indicating not only a lack of birth control but also a tacit acceptance that one or more would die young. In 1900 some 140,000 babies died in Britain before they reached their first birthday. (A century later, the figure was 5,000.) Poverty, chronic illnesses and cot deaths – some caused by smothering because of the widespread drinking habit that was more problematic before the First World War – were mostly to blame.

After the Second World War better social circumstances had an impact on infant mortality. Mothers lived longer, so more children than ever before received care in a family unit. With reduced numbers of children, there was more food to go around and the health of the young consequently improved. Fewer hours were being demanded of workers, and there was even time for days out and holidays. Families began to believe without question that their children would live to adulthood.

So parents who awoke to find their infants with stiff limbs and porcelain skin – a vibrant life force having been snatched away in the night – were left bewildered and bereft. Without symptoms, the death of a child who had been bouncing with vitality a matter of hours before filled parents with guilt, grief, questions and recriminations. There were sometimes

> During the era of *Call the Midwife*, little was known about what prompted cot deaths, which most commonly occur in babies aged between two and four months. However, for the first time, in the fifties the fate of infants was becoming a cause for public concern.

even whispers of foul play perpetuated by neighbours.

That doctors were as baffled as the families – even after an inquiry – provided scant comfort. There was a long road to travel before any of the uncertainty surrounding cot death started to clear. The acronym SIDS wasn't coined until 1969, and it wasn't until the nineties that there was finally a greater understanding of cot death.

The tragedy remains that several generations of mothers had been advised to put their babies to sleep on their stomachs, now known to be the most dangerous position. In 2005 a study published in the *International Journal of Epidemiology* looked at eighty-three pieces of advice given out to new parents in the twentieth century. It discovered that from 1940 to the mid-fifties the vast majority of texts recommended putting babies to sleep on their sides or backs.

Yet from 1954 to 1988 there was an increasing amount of guidance in favour of leaving sleeping babies on their tummies – to help with wind, reduce coughing and improve breathing. Gurus previously in favour of back sleeping, including Dr Benjamin Spock, had changed their view, saying babies on their fronts would not

FALL IN

INFANT MORTALITY

154 1900

UNDER ONE YEAR • PER THOUSAND LIVE BIRTHS

53

1938

LEE-ELLIOTT

MINISTRY OF HEALTH

choke if they were sick in the night. The opinion in favour of sleeping on stomachs wasn't universal, but it did seem influential.

In the UK the subsequent rise in the number of SIDS deaths was noted but was thought to be caused by an administrative technicality. Until 1971 deaths of this nature were attributed to respiratory problems. After SIDS was recognised as a cause of death that year, the numbers went up. But other causes of infant deaths were on the decline, and that should have rung alarm bells.

Worse still, by 1970 there was evidence from two studies that showed that the risk was statistically significantly higher to babies on the front than on the back. It must be no comfort to parents who lost children to know that there was an absence of joined-up thinking by experts in the field at the time. Even now, following a cot death, bereaved parents and medical experts are at pains to point out that there isn't always a discernible cause.

In the sixties there was a queasiness about pathology and post-mortems being carried out to push back the barriers of medical knowledge; perhaps a hangover from the Second World War when the Nazis had performed wide-ranging experiments on those in concentration camps. Afterwards, twenty doctors were charged with war crimes and crimes against humanity at the International Military Tribunal at Nuremberg, and there was evidence of grotesque activities at Dachau, Auschwitz, Buchenwald and Sachsenhausen. In July 1961 the flawed Human Tissue Act laid down guidance on the use of dead bodies for medical research that impelled inquisitive medics to be sure that no surviving relatives objected to their activities. However, ambiguity about who was in possession of the corpse led to a scandal, with hospitals storing body parts and babies' bodies for years.

By the sixties, however, childbirth was also safer than ever before, with confidential three-yearly reports revealing the top four causes of death to be toxaemia, haemorrhage, abortion (at the time carried out illegally) and pulmonary embolism – a blood clot formed in the veins of the leg suddenly blocking the arteries in the lungs.

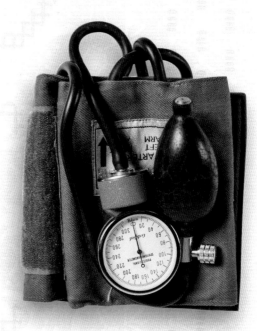

A Ministry of Health poster shows that the rates of infant mortality were tumbling fast even before the National Health Service was established, although maternal deaths were still high at the time.

Nurse Trixie Miller (Helen George)
is delighted by a baby's progress
at the clinic.

PRE-ECLAMPSIA

I DON'T LIKE TO LOSE ANYONE. That might seem a rather facile comment for a medic, but it needs to be said. Medical experience won't make the loss of a patient any less painful. Instead, it forms the cold hard stone on which we sharpen the best of ourselves. A corrective for the bluntness of our ignorance.

I'm grateful to Nurse Browne for her sharp eyes regarding Dolly Smart, Fred's daughter. I was not three feet away from her, teaching origami to the cubs and oblivious to the symptoms of toxaemia standing beside me. Dolly is now safely ensconced in the maternity home for some enforced bed rest and observation until she delivers.

Toxaemia - commonly known as pre-eclampsia - is as old as childbirth and still as deadly. There isn't much in our modern age that'll carry a pregnant mother and her child away, but toxaemia will do it. If you spot it in time, the outlook is good. Swollen feet - high blood pressure - headaches. Miss it, and things can be grim. Seizures, kidney failure, coma. Death.

Last year we missed one. Margaret Jones. New to the district, I never saw her myself, as she skipped her pre-natal clinic appointment. Nurse Miller later discovered her in seizure, and got her to the hospital. It was too late. Baby gone, and mother soon after. Nurse Miller spoke of the husband, who stayed with Mrs Jones to the end. Newlyweds, I believe. A bad business.

In the war, you'd always know when one of your men was for it. A pallor that hung over him near the end to mock your efforts. It was

rough, but there was a kind of mercy to it. An unarguable cause in the violence done by others. There is no mystery in a shrapnel wound.

Yet the causes of toxaemia still elude us. The Russians send objects into orbit miles above our heads, while on Earth the mothers and their children continue to die. The only true remedy remains the oldest – to end the pregnancy. Premature birth if necessary. Abortion if we must. A blunt knife in an age of miracles.

Yet there is a virtue in this grindstone. A sharpening of resolution; a refusal to accept our ignorance. Bringing out the best of ourselves. I don't like to lose anyone. Which means I will not be content until everyone can be saved.

Toxaemia is better known today as pre-eclampsia, and it remains a stealthy killer that suddenly transforms a commonplace pregnancy into something dangerous and scary. The first symptoms may be seemingly benign, like unexpected weight gain and a small rise in blood pressure. However, the next stage is much more serious, with headaches, visual disturbances, pains and vomiting. If the syndrome continues to gather momentum the patient will suffer convulsions and may fall into a coma, with damage to the liver, kidneys and placenta.

Medically, midwives and doctors are looking for three tell-tale symptoms during check-ups: high blood pressure, fluid retention and protein detectable in urine samples. They do not all need to be present to justify diagnosis, and sharp-eyed midwives (like Chummy) who can spot any of the signs are – literally – lifesavers.

Doctors faced with such a patient in the past had to make some tough decisions. The only remedy was to end the pregnancy promptly, hopefully in time to save the mother's life. A robust baby might survive outside the womb, as the placenta would be failing. But it might also be too small to live.

About 18 per cent of maternal deaths were caused by toxaemia by the mid-sixties, in addition to the loss of about 3,000 babies. In 1965 Robert Heading told the Royal Medical Society that the figure amounted to about half the number of people killed on Britain's roads each year, a figure that at the time was receiving swathes of publicity following the opening of a motorway network.

As it was a syndrome rather than a disease, toxaemia had to be managed rather than treated. Gloomily, Heading pointed out: 'Even with the best care available the treatment of toxaemia seems inadequate for the mid-twentieth century, and it looks as if permutations and modifications of present methods will provide nothing but trivial improvement.'

'Even with the best care available the treatment of toxaemia seems inadequate for the mid-twentieth century, and it looks as if permutations and modifications of present methods will provide nothing but trivial improvement.'

ROBERT HEADING, AT THE ROYAL MEDICAL SOCIETY, 1965

Dr. Patrick Turner

PHONE: POPLAR 491   GMC No. 89502   19 KENILWORTH ROW, E14

FOR .... DATE ....

CHAPTER 2

Miracle Drugs

19, KENILWORTH ROW
E14
POPLAR   LONDON   ....

PRESCRIPTION No. ....

When the cost conundrums of medical care that had confronted pregnant women, the elderly and the sick were finally swept away with the launch of the National Health Service, there was profound relief for many.

The necessary cash now came from taxation, with the wealthy inevitably paying more than the poor, while services were free to all users. It was a concept unknown elsewhere in the world, except perhaps in the Soviet bloc – a fact that did not endear the system to critics, as tensions escalated between East and West.

There were three main prongs to the NHS: general practitioners, hospital services and the local authority, which provided community nurses and the means to control infectious diseases, among other things. With the new system came a blizzard of paperwork for staff, with each arm of the service generating more than its fair share of bureaucracy.

As far as most people were concerned, their local doctor was the most important public face of the complex new service; men like Dr Turner were the first and often the only port of call for the general public. Family doctors tended to know their patients well, which helped when it came to assessing medical needs. They knew how underlying conditions might manifest themselves, in word or deed. Also, they had a metaphorical finger on the pulse of the local community, to further enhance that necessary personal touch.

However, GPs also had to keep abreast of fast-moving medical knowledge in order to give the best service they could,

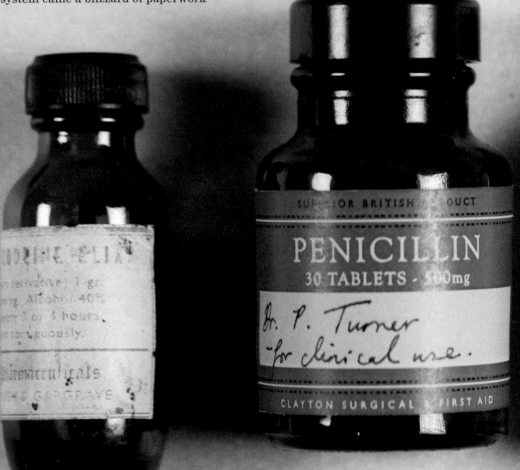

as well as orchestrate preventative work. An estimated 90 per cent of cases that came to the surgery were dealt with solely by the doctor, sometimes working in isolation. Thus the GP provided diagnosis for everything from apparently trivial complaints to serious conditions in his surgery, in clinics and small hospitals in which he had a stake. Home visits were also still a national habit in Britain, although rarely found elsewhere in the world.

In more serious or specialist cases, the doctor was the intermediary between hospital services and the patient – negotiating with both to forge a path for everyone to follow. For this reason he had to cultivate personal relationships at his local hospital in order to ease the passage of his patients; when a patient was admitted to hospital, the doctor kept in touch with ward staff to monitor their progress.

Although doctors were best placed to supervise preventive work in the community, it was this area in which their time was usually most squeezed. By now appointments lasted an average of a mere seven minutes in the winter and eleven in summer. Even so, doctors typically worked from dawn until dusk most days, while still being on call during the night. Days off were few and far between. This pressure of work was exacerbated for doctors who worked in a practice on their own.

For older GPs like Dr Turner, though, there was still a thrill in seeing a complaint that might once have proved fatal being relegated to something mundane. This was thanks to the invention of penicillin, one of the world's first antibiotics. Its story is well known but bears re-telling for the tremendous difference it made to mankind.

PENICILLIN

TODAY I VISITED NONNATUS HOUSE TO TREAT SISTER MONICA JOAN. The elderly sister had been found by police wandering on the Thames shore and has a nasty case of pneumonia to add to her increasing confusion. I've prescribed penicillin – although Sister Evangelina fears there may be a considerable gap between desired prescription and successful administration. I hear our patient regards *Penicillium Notatum* as 'waste matter' not fit for her veins. I can't argue with the narrow definition. Penicillin is, after all, derived from mould – but one must hope she can be persuaded otherwise. Medical miracles can grow in the most unlikely of places.

Pneumonia is known in these streets as the 'old people's friend' – a disease that carries off the elderly and infirm as a matter of course. Many infections were regarded with similar inevitability until the arrival of penicillin after the war. Fleming's little Petri

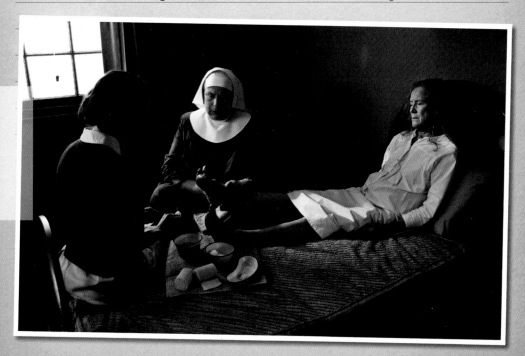

dish of waste matter showed us what a real friend medicine could be.

For those of us in the profession that experienced the dark age before penicillin - then witnessed the golden age that followed it - the memory is bittersweet. As a young doctor I saw the strong laid waste by nothing greater than a scratch from a rose thorn. I witnessed the appalling consequences of syphilis, and watched helpless as the injured soldier was poisoned by the filth in his wounds.

One case stays with me. Anzio, 1944. Lieutenant Hibbs. Fine officer and a mean centre-half. He'd fought his way up the Italian peninsula like he was the only one in the war. He took a deep graze to his knee in a regimental football match played on stone-hard Italian clay. The wound became infected. We'd heard rumours about a wonder drug for use in the big Allied push in France. In desperation I sent a telegram explaining the situation, and begging for a phial or two. The answer was kind but brief. Limited supplies - specific uses - no exceptions. I watched Hibbs fade like a flower in a vase. We buried him in a patch of hard earth.

To me, penicillin will always be associated with a form of waste matter. Yet not the substance itself - far from it. That lowly mould has done more for our world than the greatest medical minds. No, it's the countless wasted matter of humanity that preceded it. Those poor souls who were born a little too early and died a little too soon to share in Fleming's quiet miracle.

I can only hope we don't become so forgetful as to adopt Sister Monica Joan's lavish complacency in the face of such a gift. I don't think Lieutenant Hibbs would ever forgive us.

The man credited with inventing penicillin is Alexander Fleming (1881–1955). 'Flem', as he was known in the laboratory, was later described by colleague Professor Ronald Hare as 'small with blue eyes, a large head, a bent nose and a broad Ayrshire accent. Unlike his colleagues he had come from a poor home. The son of a farmer in the Scottish lowlands he had worked for a time as a clerk in a city office. He only succeeded in taking up medicine because someone left him some money.'

Conscientious with his laboratory work, Fleming was also known for his love of art and entertaining. Although he had qualified as a surgeon, he never practised. He had spent the First World War in France in a team led by Almroth Wright, investigating wound infections, and had then worked on lysozyme, effectively the antiseptic enzyme in tears.

Fleming famously returned from holiday to discover a contaminating mould in one of his Petri dishes, which appeared to be eating a nearby bacterial growth.

Later he wrote: 'When I woke up just after dawn on September 28, 1928, I certainly didn't plan to revolutionize all medicine by discovering the world's first antibiotic, or bacteria killer. But I guess that was exactly what I did.'

Analysts argued afterwards that a special set of circumstances, including the unseasonably cool weather and an open door, combined to produce the first evidence of penicillin. Certainly, Fleming struggled to reproduce the telling plate a second time. But his achievement lay in recognising that a humble mould could be so potent, and he soon knew enough to declare that it was non-toxic to animals, didn't cause undue reactions and could be used on wounds. The results were published in the *British Journal of Experimental Pathology* in June 1929.

There was a hiatus between that eureka moment, though, when Fleming realised that he'd found something that would control infection, and the production of quantities sufficient to administer to at-risk patients. No one immediately seized on the possibilities, and people continued to die from apparently trivial injuries.

Ten years later Dr Howard Florey (1898–1968), a professor of pathology at Oxford University, took a special interest in Fleming's paper about penicillin and decided to invest laboratory time in the tantalising issue of how to make more. On his team was Dr Ernst Chain (1906–1979), a Jew who had fled Nazi Germany and a key protagonist in the battle to harvest the new wonder drug. By the summer of 1940 they had liberated twenty-five mice from the scourge of blood poisoning by the administration of penicillin injections – while another twenty-five that had not received the drug had died.

The same year, when they heard about an Oxford police constable who had torn his face on a rose thorn, they had the chance to administer the drug to a patient. Albert Alexander, 48, was being consumed by infection until he was given penicillin, when he started to show signs of recovery. However, there was still not enough of the drug for long-term treatment, and – frustratingly – Alexander died.

Stung by this failure, biochemist Dr

> **Fleming famously returned from holiday to discover a contaminating mould in one of his Petri dishes, which appeared to be eating a nearby bacterial growth.**

Norman Heatley (1911–2004), who worked with Florey and Chain, constructed a makeshift factory production line but, in the face of the escalating casualties of the Second World War, the amounts produced remained pitifully small. They discovered that 1,000 specially commissioned ceramic jars stacked up at Oxford University would produce not more than a single ounce of pure penicillin. Assembling and preparing a plant in England, with its wartime shortages and increasing number of air raids, was also problematic.

In desperation, Florey and Heatley flew to America in the summer of 1941 to work with scientists in Peoria, Illinois, to resolve the problem of mass production. It was here that a laboratory assistant, Mary Hunt, brought in a cantaloupe melon covered with a golden mould that proved every bit as effective as the others, but was considerably more abundant.

There followed more trials with hospital patients, coupled with increasing levels of production, and by 1944 the drug firm Pfizer had taken on the commercial challenge.

It wasn't just blood poisoning that penicillin acted against. It gave remarkable results when dealing with pneumonia, too. The symptoms include a high temperature, shortness of breath, a cough and even confusion. Although anyone can catch it, the elderly and the very young are most susceptible, along with those suffering with pre-existing medical conditions.

Pneumonia is caused by an inflammation of the lungs, often but not exclusively initiated by a bacterium called *Streptococcus pneumoniae*. It can be treated with penicillin, as well as rest and drinking plenty of water. During the First World War, the death rate from bacterial pneumonia was 18 per cent. That figure was cut in the Second World War to less than 1 per cent, thanks largely to miracle drugs such as penicillin. Its effect on the battlefield against injuries and illness among servicemen was far-reaching. It is therefore unsurprising that Fleming, Florey and Chain were jointly awarded the Nobel Prize in Physiology or Medicine in 1945 'for the discovery of penicillin and its curative effect in various infectious diseases'. Fleming and Florey were also knighted. Forty-five years later, the oversight regarding Heatley's contribution was partially corrected when he was given Oxford's first honorary doctorate of medicine.

Following the war, there was some ill-feeling about the idea that Britain had given away one of the world's most pivotal discoveries for a pittance – and was then forced to buy it back from American companies. According to Britain's *News Chronicle* of 29 August 1949: 'Our scientists lack the resources of their American colleagues for systematically exploring the vast range of moulds and micro-organisms for the discovery of new species with new disease-attacking properties and our commercial concerns lag behind in the technology of this field.

'A sad commentary on all this is the experience of Professor Ernest Chain ... [who] has gone to Rome University where the Italian government has given him facilities which for seven years he has been trying to obtain for scientists in this country'.

In 1971, aged seven, I was confined to an oxygen tent in a Liverpool hospital as I battled pneumonia. Soaked in sweat from the effects of the plastic tent in the warm hospital environment, my discomfort was significantly increased by the sight of a nurse arriving to give another of my thrice-daily injections. But today my main memory is not of the pain in my pin-cushion bottom, but the sight of my father at my bedside throughout the ordeal. He smiled encouragement, his old commando's eyes shining with a rarely seen faith. "It's penicillin, son," he said. "It will make you

The success story of penicillin is one that remains close to my heart. As a twenty-year-old, my commando father, Joe, was one of the first on Gold Beach on France's northern coast in the grey dawn of 6 June 1944, when the Allies began to wrest Europe from Hitler's control. Like many in that first wave on D-Day my father was injured as he headed for the safety of a sea wall. A German stick grenade tossed in his direction left him with fifty shrapnel wounds down his left side.

He was transported back to England with hundreds of other injured servicemen, in his case to Leicester Royal Infirmary. When once he would have been cleaned up and made comfortable as staff waited helplessly for nature to take its course, he and others were for the first time given penicillin to rally their bodies' natural defences and ward off the inevitable sepsis that followed in the wake of war wounds. He told me how they all huddled around the beds, showing each other their healing wounds.

As the days went by, my father described the wonder of seeing his own shrapnel scars recede. Penicillin saved his life.

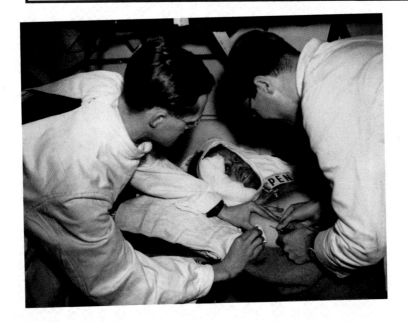

A soldier injured during the aftermath of the D-Day invasion gets a life-preserving shot of penicillin from doctors finally armed with weapons to stop the march of harmful bacteria.

better again, I promise." It's the way he said that word, 'penicillin'. Like a sacred thing; a scientific miracle. He was right. It did make me better. And even now I still can't say the word without seeing my father's face. Without it, my father would not have lived long enough to have had me. And if I hadn't been treated with it as a child I wouldn't be able to talk about his love today.

Back in the doctor's surgery at the close of the fifties, the availability of penicillin meant that doctors could treat more patients in a single surgery visit than ever before. Alongside that, there were more off-the-shelf treatments to be prescribed. From 1958 there was also effective treatment for blood pressure, for example, among other lower-grade conditions that had plagued patients.

Penicillin played its part in cutting the number of deaths related to childbirth, too. However, it was preceded by other treatments that had themselves been trail-blazers. Drugs in the sulphonamide family, an early antibiotic in use from the thirties, finally helped to reduce maternal deaths, which had stayed stubbornly at levels known in Victorian England. Pioneered in Germany, these drugs were used by both sides during the Second World War, but were ultimately eclipsed by the more versatile penicillin.

Penicillin was also responsible for reducing the numbers who died from puerperal fever, also known as childbed fever. This was an infection picked up during childbirth that brought about poor appetite, a temperature and lethargy, and claimed numerous lives before the fundamentals of infection control were understood.

The plant-based drug ergometrine, used to stimulate the delivery of the placenta, also became available to obstetricians and midwives in the thirties, although the properties of the plants involved in its production had been guessed at for many years before by herbalists. Thanks to its effect on the blood vessels, it helps to stop uterine bleeding after childbirth. A decade later the naturally occurring oxytocin became available in drug form, which helped to quicken labour and reduce bleeding. By the fifties this was widely in use – another invaluable weapon in the armoury of medics like Dr Turner.

WASH YOUR HANDS

There was a time – not that long ago – when even basic hand washing wasn't routinely carried out by those attending a birth. The man who helped changed this was Hungarian Dr Ignaz Semmelweis (1818–1865), who saw how women who had their babies with doctors or medical students in attendance were more likely to die than those attended by midwives.

He realised that those same doctors and students had often come straight to the mother's bedside from the dissection of corpses in another part of the hospital and, as was the norm, didn't wash their hands or change their clothes in between. Dr Semmelweis proved his suspicions by instituting a hand-washing policy among staff. He achieved a substantial cut in mortality rates, which was further enhanced when he made sure the instruments being used were also cleaned. There were, of course, no sinks with taps that gushed with clean running water at the time, so basic hygiene was something of a challenge.

Not everyone was convinced even then, with critics believing that disease was borne via a miasma, or 'bad air', and that a new ventilation system at the hospital was responsible for bringing about the improvements.

Unfortunately, despite the profound good sense he exhibited during his career, Dr Semmelweis was committed to an insane asylum with what was probably early-onset Alzheimer's disease. He died there after being beaten by staff. Despite his persuasive findings, maternal death rates were only reduced in hospitals; the message didn't immediately filter through to midwives working in the home.

Apart from the miasma theory, there was also a belief that malnutrition was the cause of maternal deaths, which persisted into the thirties. Accordingly, one medical officer of health in South Wales – where maternal death rates were high – remarked that the region needed a herd of cows rather than a herd of obstetricians. Soon evidence from industrial Rochdale in Lancashire proved him wrong. It was here that the excessive levels of deaths in new mums were being recorded. With its population of under-privileged and malnourished families, the idea that poor nutrition played a role seemed to be borne out. However, the arrival of an energetic medical officer galvanised those in the field to raise standards and, although the deprivation remained the same, the number of maternal deaths was slashed from double the national average to well below half.

Meanwhile, a much later study of a faith group in America comprising healthy, middle-class followers revealed vastly scaled-up rates of maternal deaths after women declined medical expertise during childbirth. Proof, if it were needed, that hygiene was key.

PURE

SURGICA
SPIRIT

B.P.C.   No. 1

TO PREVENT BED SORE
APPLY WITH A PAD O
COTTON WOOL

FOR EXTERNAL USE

Dr. Patrick Turner

PHONE: POPLAR 491	GMC No. 89502	19 KENILWORTH ROW, E14

FOR .... DATE ....

CHAPTER 3

Losers in Poplar's Lottery of Life

19, KENILWORTH ROW
E14
POPLAR   LONDON   ....

PRESCRIPTION No.

THACKRAY
SUTURSILK
No. B/.004   25 yds.
A WATERPROOF, SERUMPROOF
SUTURE SILK.
May be boiled or
steam sterilised.
CHAS. F. THACKRAY LTD., LEEDS & LONDON

CARE OF THE ELDERLY

A 'LAND FIT FOR HEROES' IS A BARREN PLACE IF IT
CAN'T MAKE HEROES OF ITS MOST VULNERABLE. When I
began in Poplar the war was barely over, and we still scrambled over
bomb-blown rubble to reach our patients. Yet there was promise in the
air; a new hope to leaven the austerity. The National Assistance Act
had blown away the last vestiges of ancient Poor Laws. For the first
time we could reach those last untouchables - the ones we'd forsaken
for centuries in vile workhouses and infirmaries.

The most elderly of these had endured terrible hardship. The last
workhouses had shut their doors in the thirties, yet the detritus of
these cruel places still fell into the cracks in our society: lost
somewhere between the limits of our charity and their own misfortune.

Dignity restored:
Mrs Jenkins is included in
the Christmas preparations.

They could be found in filthy hovels, or sleeping rough - minds infirm and clothes crawling with lice.

The Nonnatuns recently brought a tragic case to my attention. Mary Anne Jenkins. Mrs Jenkins is a widowed veteran of the workhouse. I was sent to a slum near the docks to check on her welfare.

It's the smell that lingers. The stench of sustained self-neglect resulting from the abandonment of hope. The foul-sweet odour of defecation, sickness and decline: poverty's perfume. As a doctor one learns to hold the breath and fix the attention on the subject of a curse, not on the olfactory outcome of their punishment. The room was in an appalling state. Mrs Jenkins was huddled at one end in rags. As I approached to help, she screamed - a cornered animal, expecting only harm.

Timothy still hasn't forgiven me for snatching his fish and chips to feed her with. He's a little too young to understand. She took each mouthful anxiously - protecting it from unseen enemies. The sight shamed me to my core. I determined that the next help I brought would not come wrapped in old newspaper, but would represent the steady payment of a debt.

Clothing, cleanliness, food. Warmth for winter. Medicine for angina, and nurses to dispense it. Spectacles to see the world and a hearing aid to hear its long apology. The relief of pain and the possibility of trust. The chance to grieve, and the means to live beyond grief.

Compassion isn't just a moment's sentiment - a lachrymose song played on a pub piano and soon forgotten. True compassion is

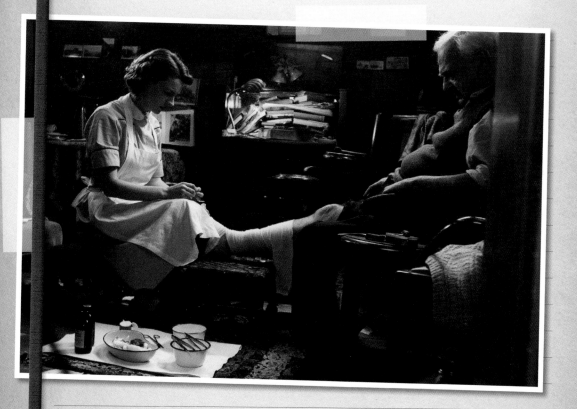

architecture. It is structured and planned and built and sustained over decades. The elderly are hostages to the realities of our present. They cannot trade privation for the hope of some distant, better future. What their life amounts to is a cold summation of our own humanity. If we do not care, then they will fail. If we do, then they will prosper.

She will prosper. Or else there are no heroes in this land worth the name.

> *If we do not care, then they will fail.*
> *If we do, then they will prosper.*

Family doctors considered themselves poorly paid during the *Call the Midwife* era – and with some justification, thanks to a historical quirk linked to costs.

During a thirty-five-year career, a GP was estimated to earn £79,000 according to figures produced in 1956; less than a hospital doctor, who could earn £100,000, and considerably less than the £117,000 a consultant might expect. The figure recommended by government advisors was £102,000. A GP's earnings were therefore below those that a barrister or solicitor might expect, but greater than those of an architect, accountant or university lecturer.

Nor did GPs pocket all their earnings, as payments for staff, premises and equipment came out of their gross salary. Ideally, a doctor's practice needed someone with secretarial experience who could manage a well-run appointments system, so he needed to recruit at least one assistant. A modern practice also required accommodation for local authority staff such as health visitors, and separate examination rooms.

When he was Minister for Health in 1963, Enoch Powell explained the difficulty: 'The more a doctor decides to spend on his premises or the staffing of his practice, the less his individual net income becomes, and vice versa.' Consequently, many family doctors ended up working from home. It was thought that this financial wrinkle caused a shortage of new applicants, as in 1962 fewer than 15 per cent of GPs were aged under 35.

One initiative the government ran to counteract this problem was to offer loans, so that doctors could improve their premises without dipping into their savings. In 1961 what money was available for such projects was earmarked only for group practices and two-man rural outposts.

For some doctors there were opportunities to enhance pay. They often worked outside their general practice: as police surgeons, on hospital boards, for the armed services, in industry and for a broad variety of charitable projects.

However, there were also other hurdles along a GP's career path. There was little glamour involved in tending to the succession of minor ailments paraded in the waiting room. There might be cases of scabies, intestinal worms, whooping cough, sexually transmitted diseases and the like. Younger doctors hoped for more exciting work, while the old hands tried not to be ground down by the mundanity of issuing repeat prescriptions. Perhaps this helps to explain the fact that the number of students entering medicine as a whole in 1959 dropped by more than 2 per cent.

As far as working conditions were concerned, Metropolitan doctors had a special cause for complaint, as at the end of the war they were working in more difficult circumstances than most. Cities, especially London, had taken a pounding from the Luftwaffe. During the Blitz of 1940, German bombers had targeted the capital for 57 consecutive nights in an attempt to flatten homes and industries, and destroy morale. Poplar was in close proximity to the East India Docks – a perpetual target – and almost a quarter of its buildings had been obliterated or severely damaged. Even before hostilities had finished there were plans to rebuild, but money was in short supply. Although there was some rebuilding work carried out almost immediately and a host of prefabricated buildings put up, rubble-strewn bombsites and roofless houses were a common sight for years afterwards.

The peace-time journey back to normality would be a long one, and was marked by some significant events orchestrated to redefine the capital. When London hosted the 1948 Olympic Games,

King George VI and Queen Elizabeth visited Poplar's Lansbury Estate in 1950, built in preparation for the Festival of Britain.

As far as working conditions were concerned, Metropolitan doctors had a special cause for complaint, as at the end of the war they were working in more difficult circumstances than most. Cities, especially London, had taken a pounding.

they were dubbed 'the austerity games', with the only sponsored kit being 600 pairs of Y-fronts. A total of 4,100 athletes – 90 per cent of them male – from fifty-nine countries took part. Although the men stayed in military camps and women competitors were in London colleges, they were provided with extra food rations to help enhance their performance.

In 1951, six years after the end of the war, the Festival of Britain was opened, marking the centenary of an exhibition that had helped transform Victorian England by trumpeting its scientific achievements. This time it was the nation's resilience that was being celebrated, and there was a growing sense of affluence, although rationing of some food items was still in force and reconstruction efforts were slow. Along with London's Royal Festival Hall, the Lansbury Estate in

With the first phase of the Lansbury Estate, opened for the Festival of Britain, just 1,197 homes were created.

Poplar was built. Its purpose, apart from providing much-needed housing, was as the Live Architecture Exhibition, a key component of the Festival. It was named after George Lansbury (1859–1940), a radical socialist politician from Poplar. Given the financial and time constraints, the building produced for the Festival was only the first phase of the project. But Lansbury housing was designed to provide more than 1,000 people with a home that included an internal bathroom and toilet – for some, the first time they had experienced such luxury. Alice and Albert Snoddy and their two children were the first residents to move in, on 14 February 1951. Others followed with mixed emotions, reluctant to leave close-knit communities despite a substantial upgrade in the quality of their living accommodation.

Among architects, the reception to the estate was also muted, with a feeling that it was worthy but dull, and that an opportunity had been missed. However, one eminent fan was American writer and critic Lewis Mumford. Writing in *The New Yorker* in 1953, he declared: 'I shall be surprised if Lansbury is not one of the best bits of housing and urban planning anywhere.'

Whatever the merits or otherwise of the Lansbury Estate, even the most cynical would have agreed that it was a positive development compared with other housing of the time. Despite the wholesale social improvements introduced after the Second World War, there were still plentiful examples of squalor in Poplar and elsewhere, all too frequently inhabited by the elderly and the confused.

Years before Imperialist Cecil Rhodes declared that to be English was 'to have won the first prize in the lottery of life', there were many who had cause to disagree. Before the advent of the welfare state, the outlook for older people who

> Lansbury housing was designed to provide more than 1,000 people with a home that included an internal bathroom and toilet – for some, the first time they had experienced such luxury.

didn't have the benefit of a private income or an inclusive family was bleak. For them, poverty and homelessness held special terrors; anyone who turned sixty-five in 1958 might well have spent their formative years in a workhouse, a solution to the plight of the poor favoured in Victorian times. At the very least they would have witnessed the plight of those who did.

Poor relief in Britain had existed for centuries. But the evolution of the workhouse chimed with warped Victorian values which shaped a well-meaning intention into something of a nightmare. The aim was to provide food and shelter – and later medical attention and education – to society's poor, who were liable to be left destitute if they lost their jobs. That was laudable enough, but a desire to see gratitude expressed in terms of hard work and humility had families segregated on arrival, sleeping in filthy dormitory conditions and eating, for the most part, skilly, or gruel.

During the day men, women and children laboured quietly and hard on treadmills crushing corn, doing domestic chores or picking oakum, a job that was also assigned to convicts at the time. It involved tugging into shreds rope from ships that was stiff with salt and tar. Once it was fluffy again, the material was used

Anyone who turned sixty-five in 1958 might well have spent their formative years in a workhouse, a solution to the plight of the poor favoured in Victorian times. At the very least they would have witnessed the plight of those who did.

both for making new rope and in the seams of new ships. Thus the paupers earned their keep.

Those who went to the workhouse did so voluntarily, seeking leave from a local relieving officer before gaining entry. It was an indication of just how desperate things were for them at the time. They could also depart at any time, although it was an offence to be outside the workhouse in its uniform – issued clothing usually held in place by string. In reality they had few options.

Ultimately the system bore the appearance of being a punishment for 'idle malingerers' rather than assistance for the poor, and any link with the workhouse was perceived as a disgrace. Those destined to spend nights, weeks or years there were also trapped by the negligible pay they received.

Later, conditions improved, with the Poplar workhouse operating a farm in Essex to provide more meaningful work for its male residents. Progress had come late in the day, however, and only as the result of some concerted campaigning.

On the Board of Guardians that operated the Poplar workhouse was Will Crooks (1852–1921), who had himself been a resident as a child after his father lost an arm in an accident and his seamstress mother could not earn enough to keep seven children. After escaping the confines of the workhouse Crooks received an education, despite the penny a week it cost his hard-pressed, illiterate mother. Later he worked on the docks, where he fought through trade unionism for the underprivileged and raised funds during the 1889 London Dock Strike. A gifted orator, he helped form the Labour Party and was the first working-class member of the Poplar Board of Guardians, becoming Chair in 1897.

A lifelong resident of Poplar, its one-time mayor and an MP for Woolwich, Crooks worked with George Lansbury to lessen the severity of the workhouse surroundings. On one visit he found people in dire need of clothes and boots, rat droppings in the skilly and a considerable number of residents contriving to go to prison, where they were sure conditions would be preferable. He shared his findings with an official inquiry conducted by the Poor Law Commission in 1906.

Workhouses were finally abolished in 1929. However, the buildings were renamed Public Assistance Institutions and remained in use; they still instilled fear among those on the outside struggling with the economic hardships brought about by a worldwide depression, who knew they were destined for a joyless existence and a comfortless environment should they be swept up in that era's welfare system. Inside there were increasing numbers of people who were failing with age, all institutionalised after spending years adhering to the cloistered discipline the workhouses provided. How they would fare without close supervision was anybody's guess. Only after the NHS was properly established were most institutions of this nature finally closed, with many going on to have a new identity as a hospital.

At the turn of the 20th century, Poplar Union Workhouse was the area's answer to welfare problems. Campaigners later found inmates were being deprived of food, proper clothing, warmth – and dignity.

Workhouses were finally abolished in 1929. However, the buildings were renamed Public Assistance Institutions and remained in use; they still instilled fear among those on the outside struggling with the economic hardships brought about by a worldwide depression, who knew they were destined for a joyless existence and a comfortless environment should they be swept up in that era's welfare system.

RICKETS

I SAW BRENDA MCENTIE AT ANTENATAL CLINIC TODAY.
It's been a while. Brenda had rickets as a child, and the resulting deformity of her pelvis led to four unsuccessful pregnancies. She now has a new husband and a new opportunity for motherhood. The Health Service can now extract her child surgically and safely - yet I fear Brenda's past experiences might prove harder to dislodge.

Rickets is something I see less and less these days, though it was quite a common thing when I first arrived in Poplar. It's an example of how tenacious an enemy to health poverty can be. Rickets feeds on purely social ills - the bad diet and sunless lives of the poor. Yet the consequences are all too physical: crippling the innocent and attacking our most young and vulnerable, even a generation later.

Yet maybe I find it too easy to forget the grip that such a physical affliction can maintain on the mind of someone affected. Today I was given a gentle, if noisy, reminder.

There was a new nurse-midwife at the clinic today called Browne. The other girls call her Chummy. Rather a tall woman - pleasant and keen, but a little nervous. When Mrs McEntie was admitted, I informed Nurse Browne of Brenda's past losses, and how a surgical delivery would eradicate the risk that her condition had posed to past births. To my surprise, Mrs McEntie became distressed and tearful. She had

Rickets feeds on purely social ills — the bad diet and sunless lives of the poor

felt her baby move, and this brought back memories of similar moments in her earlier pregnancies when she had subsequently lost her child. It had been careless and insensitive of me. Yet I was impressed by the way Nurse Browne reassured her – and how this also seemed to help the new nurse find her confidence.

Unfortunately, the moment of affirmation was shattered by an accident involving Nurse Browne, the cubicle curtain and a trolley full of equipment. Sister Evangelina's expression reminded me of a pugnacious regimental bulldog that I'd once had the misfortune to offend.

I caught up with Nurse Browne in the kitchen on my break. She was shovelling the remains of her accident into the bin, and looking rather sheepish. I complimented her on her treatment of our patient and assured her that the primary aim of medicine is to *care*, and not simply to treat. She seemed reassured. I do hope so. She will make a fine nurse and a wonderful midwife.

I also hope Brenda sleeps a little easier tonight, thanks to Nurse Browne's insightful intervention – and in spite of my own insensitivity. Nurse Browne might have had the accident, but I fear I'd been the clumsier one.

Sister Evangelina (Pam Ferris)

In 1934 East Poplar borough council proposed to fix cages to tenement windows so that children could safely benefit from fresh air and sunshine.

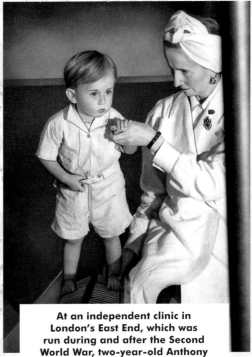

At an independent clinic in London's East End, which was run during and after the Second World War, two-year-old Anthony Bull, suffering from rickets, walks up a corrugated ladder to help strengthen his legs.

Inner-city GPs like Dr Turner saw a range of different maladies, some of which belonged to the same bygone era as the workhouse. Rickets was in a similar bracket of diseases as scurvy and beri-beri; brought about by poor nutrition, it was little understood until the early twentieth century. Indeed, the word 'vitamin' wasn't coined until after 1912, when Polish-born scientist Casimir Funk recognised that important chemical nutrients hitherto unrecognised were probably responsible for improved health. He called these 'vital amines'.

Various Nobel prizes were awarded through the first half of the twentieth century for work by scientists linked to vitamins A, B, C and D. It was vitamin D that was crucial in the treatment and prevention of rickets, and this could be taken into the body via food and sunshine. Without it, the calcium and phosphates necessary for bone growth are inhibited. Until the link between vitamin D and rickets was made, many children suffered from bow legs, curved spines, pigeon chests and thickening around the wrists and ankles. Deficiency meant painful muscles and feeble bones. Poor or restricted diets coupled with a lack of sunlight in industrial areas caused by clouds of smoke were the primary causes of rickets. Girls suffered more than boys, as they were often detained at home to look after younger siblings while boys played outside, where they could top up on vitamin D via the sun's rays.

Years previously, when rickets had been observed among the rich as well as the poor, there were prescribed rules about diet that failed to encourage the intake of foods that would hinder the spread of the disease, such as oily fish, milk and eggs. No one had any idea that something as natural as sunshine could prevent bones becoming so soft that they buckled.

CONCENTRATED

ORANGE JUICE

THE CONCENTRATED JUICE OF NINE FRESH ORANGES

Concentrated orange juice is now available without tokens for all children up to five years old at 1/6 per bottle. It is excellent value because:

Each bottle contains as much Vitamin C as 9 good-sized oranges, and costs less;

The concentrated juice, blended from specially selected sun-ripe oranges, is more digestible for very young children;

Orange juice helps the development of young children and the Vitamin C is essential for their health.

Expectant mothers should get it too . . . it's important

LOOK FOR THIS '9 SUN-RIPE ORANGES' LABEL ON THE BOTTLES AT YOUR NEAREST CLINIC OR WELFARE FOODS DISTRIBUTION POINT.

WELFARE FOODS SERVICE   Issued by the Ministry of Health.

After vitamin D in its various forms was identified and isolated in laboratories in the thirties there was at last hope for young sufferers, and also those afflicted by the adult form of the disease, known as osteomalacia.

From 1944 the British government issued free milk to schoolchildren, and with the inception of the NHS came the opportunity for children to have regular orange juice – rich in vitamin C, which helps wounds to heal and keeps cells healthy – and cod liver oil. The latter may have made numerous children gag with its viscous fishiness, but it also helped to eradicate rickets in Britain.

Poor or restricted diets coupled with a lack of sunlight in industrial areas caused by clouds of smoke were the primary causes of rickets.

Dr. Patrick Turner

PHONE: POPLAR 491   GMC No. 89502   19 KENILWORTH ROW, E14

FOR .... DATE ....

CHAPTER 4

Fragile Lives and Lost Hopes

19, KENILWORTH ROW
E14
POPLAR   LONDON ....

PRESCRIPTION No. ....

rior to the advent of trained midwives, there were women who would regularly attend births in their neighbourhood; some were a godsend – known as 'wise women', with literally years of experience to hand – while others were a health hazard. Even those who charged cash for their services could not be presumed to be doing a good and safe job.

Midwifery wasn't recognised as a 'proper job' until the passing of the Midwives Act in 1902, which helped to perpetuate the training already in existence. Still, the services of a midwife were not free unless she chose to work for nothing.

Before the Second World War access to a GP had been free to low-paid workers thanks to the 1911 National Insurance Act, but not necessarily to their wives or families. Nor did it come without cost for better-paid people and the retired. Nonetheless this act, borrowed from existing German legislation and coupled with the Old-Age Pensions Act of 1908, did begin laying the foundations for people's welfare and included some maternity benefit and disability allowance.

There was a growing recognition that the health of the nation was vitally important and was linked to its general well-being. It became a headline issue when army recruiters at the turn of the century found that significant numbers of volunteers were too sick to be admitted to its ranks, at a time when Britain was embroiled in the Boer War.

The School Medical Service was formed in 1907 to help address childhood conditions, and in 1919 a Ministry of Health was established for the first time to raise the bar for everyone, nationwide. For those who fell outside the state's welfare bracket, there was often a charitable fund ready to foot the bills, usually run by friendly societies. The use of these funds meant that doctors were paid only a bare minimum, and they had to rely on wealthier patients to make up any shortfall in their income. There was therefore little incentive to invest in equipment or investigate new ways of tackling disease.

That all changed with the arrival of the NHS. It came along with great strides forward in science and brought health to the forefront of everyone's mind.

Midwifery wasn't recognised as a 'proper job' until the passing of the Midwives Act in 1902.

THE BIRTH OF THE NHS

By 1958 the NHS had been in existence for a decade, offering everyone care 'from womb to tomb' without charge. Fears that it would be inflexible or cost too much money hadn't been realised. Surveys proved that it was popular, with almost everybody wanting it to continue.

Previously, when he was health minister, Aneurin Bevan had observed that the volume of need that became apparent after the creation of the NHS was a sign of the 'silent suffering' that had existed beforehand. For example, women suffered the indignities of a prolapsed womb before free health care, rather than seek costly medical assistance.

However, the creation of the NHS left family doctors with a broad and perpetually evolving workload, thanks to a booming birth rate, more children surviving childhood ailments, fewer women dying in childbirth and people living longer than ever before. Although they were on the front line of the fight against ill-health – and were winning more battles than ever before – GPs felt overworked and underpaid. A loyalty to the health of their patients shackled most to their post for increasingly long hours.

Of course, the NHS didn't create community doctors. There had for centuries been physicians, apothecaries and surgeons at work, with varying degrees of skill and success. Early in the eighteenth century there were the first signs of structure for those working for the better health of their fellows, with the Apothecaries Act of 1815 acting as a focus for those in the field. The term 'general practitioner' first appeared in 1823, and nine years later the British Medical Association was formed.

But it was in the twentieth century that public health awareness came to the fore, with the benefits of education and application amply illustrated in a number of campaigns that cut the numerous instances of previously fatal diseases and improved the outlook for unborn children and their mothers. The advent of a defined midwifery service was a crucial part of this.

Perhaps it was no surprise that having a hospital birth seemed to gain greater currency with every passing year, as mothers sought to eliminate the element of the unexpected. This didn't necessarily mean going to the impersonal general hospital, though, as many GPs had a number of beds at their disposal, providing a more intimate environment but with greater access to medical equipment than was available at home births. This was a concept that would not survive, but the loss of GP maternity hospitals on grounds of safety and cost has since been hotly contested.

There was nothing uniform about GP maternity units, other than the principle that it was critical to have those beds close to the family home, given the length of time for which new mothers were expected to stay in hospital. Some stood alone, while others were attached to the general hospital and so had ready access to the skills of a consultant should they be needed. There were also GP maternity units attached to midwifery hospitals and at cottage hospitals; however, those established away from general hospitals tended to be in older, inappropriate accommodation.

While the size of GP maternity units varied from two to fifty beds, the average number of beds in each unit was thirteen. Sometimes the doctors delivered babies there. Often it was midwives with the doctor present. All units were equipped with gas and air machines by the sixties, as well as other systems of pain relief. If there was no consultant obstetrician on hand then the 'flying squad' could be called. Established in 1935 and used also for home births, this comprised skilled and equipped staff who could speed their way to any labour emergency, once summoned.

In 1959 there were a total of 19,781 maternity beds in Britain, of which some 3,500 – or 17 per cent – were GP beds.

Having a hospital birth seemed to gain greater currency with every passing year.

A report into GP maternity units was conducted between 1960 and 1962 and found some praiseworthy elements, but an underlying agenda to move maternity services towards general hospitals with access to a consultant was clear.

'In many of these units it is a matter of pride that no woman is ever refused a bed, hence periodic overcrowding occurs in accommodation often inadequate even for the established number of beds.

'Many of the practitioners in these units are men of great experience and no doubt many have considerable competence and skill and achieve good results. But as records are often incomplete and no figures are collated, there is no real evidence to prove whether the work done in units with no consultant supervision is as well done as in others with varying degrees of consultant control.

'At the same time there are instances of omissions and practices not in accord with accepted standards of good obstetric care.'

There was, the report said, great difficulty in staffing GP maternity units. 'In one region in 1960 two units had to be closed completely for lack of staff, another had to close to enable the staff to have a holiday, a new unit of ten beds completed in 1959 could not be opened for lack of staff, another unit has kept going by unofficial help from the Domiciliary Midwifery Service. Only ten beds of a 20-bed unit in the same region are in use, the midwifery staff consisting of matron, two agency midwives and a part-time midwife ... when the midwife on duty has

Hospital births meant a lengthy ward stay. The ten-day period of 'lying-in' was valued by some women as a time for rest and recuperation and resented by others who wanted to get back to their homes and families.

to accompany an emergency transfer to a consultant hospital the unit may be left without trained staff.'

There was also a growing focus on the comparative costs of small, GP-run units. One study in Northumberland of five maternity units reveals that in 1960 a hospital unit with a consultant was the cheapest option, costing £31 19s 4d per patient, while an isolated GP unit was the most expensive, at £34 11s 7d per patient.

In conclusion, the report into GP maternity units said: '[The units] suffer from many handicaps such as uneconomic size ... poor premises and a serious shortage of midwives.

'High transfer rates in labour reflect initial poor selection of cases. The staff of the unit sometimes have no knowledge of the patients' antenatal history. There are no figures by which the quality of care in GP units can be assessed, but evidence given to the Maternity Services Committee indicated that where beds were supervised in close liaison with the hospital and where there was a strict selection of cases, the maternal and perinatal mortality rates were much better than in units which had no supervision.'

Still, among doctors there was an argument that the existence of GP hospitals helped to raise standards.

Such hospitals attracted the best young doctors, as obstetric work held great appeal for young medics. A GP's practice was enhanced if it could offer maternity beds and the continuity of care that accompanied them, and would be less attractive to new doctors without it.

There were 3,656 GP maternity beds available in 1960, with an average occupancy of 2,654 – so they were just about three-quarters filled, at a time when childbirth for British women was poised to undergo a major transformation.

Hospital births meant a lengthy ward stay. The ten-day period of 'lying-in' was valued by some women as a time for rest and recuperation and resented by others who wanted to get back to their homes and families. Yet the issue was more political than it at first seemed, because it was linked to a welfare payment given to mums.

At the time all mothers got the maternity grant, which stood at £16 by 1964. However, those mothers who had babies at home were entitled to a home confinement grant of £6, introduced in 1953 to help towards the extra expenses they incurred. Women planning to have their babies at home but ferried into hospital at the last minute were later included in payments of the home confinement grant.

Soon anyone who stayed in hospital for a matter of hours or days was agitating to receive extra cash. But future prime minister Margaret Thatcher, at the time responsible for the issue at the Ministry of Pensions and National Insurance, was reluctant to make changes, asserting that some mothers would always miss out by virtue of bad timing. Working mothers who paid National Insurance also received a weekly allowance of £3 7s 6d a week for 18 weeks and this, she reasoned, was sufficient.

In 1961 there were 534,500 hospital confinements. Of those, just 4,250 were discharged on the same day and fewer than 15 per cent of mothers went home within five days. Meanwhile, other evidence pointed to the apparent advisability for women to go to general hospitals to give birth rather than stay in the comfort of their own homes.

In 1958 the National Birthday Trust Fund, formed in 1928 and one of the country's oldest health charities, surveyed every birth taking place during the week beginning 3 March.

Unsurprisingly it took months to properly analyse the 17,000 detailed records gathered.

When the results were presented in 1962 they seemed to show a troubling picture. The death rate of babies among middle-class families was half that of those languishing with lower incomes. And crucially, it seemed that well-off women were more likely to give birth in hospital or GP maternity units than their working-class counterparts. Midwives and GPs who supported home confinements were left reeling by the findings, and many began questioning the faith they had maintained in the system of home births.

Their views were shaped still further by a confidential inquiry into maternal deaths in the early sixties which found that in some cases, arranging for home confinement or birth in a small maternity home was 'unwise', and that it 'contributed largely to the patient's death would appear certain'. This was the stark message disseminated by those 'in the know'.

One of the final blows to those who supported home birth was a report in 1967 by the Maternity and Midwifery Advisory Committee, chaired by John Peel, which recommended that 100 per cent of women gave birth in hospital. Soon home births and GP maternity hospitals would be largely consigned to history as babies were, as a matter of course, born in general hospitals. Even so, nobody could be made to go into hospital, and midwives could not refuse care.

The expectation that all women would go to hospital for childbirth was bolstered by the development of antenatal care, which was transformed in the seventies – particularly with the arrival of ultrasound scans, which meant that the arrival of twins could at last be properly predicted. Women were thus ushered into hospitals from an early stage in their pregnancies, normalising visits there.

From 1968 there was electronic foetal monitoring on offer during labour, and women became used to taking advantage of the technology now attached to the business of childbirth. By 1975 just 5 per cent of births took place at home.

However, the wholesale move into hospitals also changed the way women were being treated. In 1970 the National Birthday Trust Fund again looked at every birth that took place in a single nominated week – and compared the figures with those gathered in 1958. It found that the number of inductions, Caesareans and episiotomies had increased markedly. In fact, the rate of inductions accelerated from 15 per cent in 1965 to 41 per cent in 1974, with critics convinced that the

Soon home births and GP maternity hospitals would be largely consigned to history as babies were, as a matter of course, born in general hospitals. Even so, nobody could be made to go into hospital, and midwives could not refuse care.

process led to more painful labours, increased use of pain-relief and the need for more interventions by instruments, or operations. At the time the most midwives would do to induce a birth was to recommend a long hot bath, a dose of castor oil and an enema.

Episiotomies were also a concern, as what was once considered an emergency procedure had clearly become routine. In little more than a decade the practice of obstetrics had changed into an art of intervention. Yet still doctors relied on an ancient tool that had assisted in births for centuries, once hidden from labouring women in order not to alarm them.

For decades, the outlook for women and babies enduring a difficult, drawn-out pregnancy had been bleak. Should the infant fail to appear promptly options were few, and those attending the birth had some hard decisions to make: should they let the labour run its course, or remove the foetus by whatever means possible in a bid to save a struggling woman's life? If they chose the latter course then the baby was destroyed by the use of jabbing hooks and needles, and removed in pieces. With poor standards of hygiene and a lack of understanding of infection, the removal of the foetus did not guarantee the survival of the mother.

It took centuries before the study of obstetrics was sufficiently organised to help. There were two outstanding innovations in the story of childbirth, one of which is considerably more popular today than the other.

The first was forceps – the invention of a family of French Protestants who had fled to England. The Chamberlens were a colourful dynasty, with father William calling two sons by the same name. Peter 'the elder' (1560–1631) is thought to have designed the forceps that were later used during a miscarriage suffered by Queen Henrietta Maria, wife of the ill-fated Charles I. Peter 'the younger' (1572–1626), known for his flamboyant dress sense, was, like his brother, effectively a midwife. At the time it was far more common for there to be male birth attendants, although the fashion for an *accoucheur* was more noticeable in France.

Both Peters were members of the Barber-Surgeons Company and together they fell out with the College of Physicians. They were the jealous keepers of an ingenious long-handled contraption that could lift or pull out a baby trapped in the birth canal by gripping its head. A son of Peter 'the younger', called Hugh, continued the tradition, and shielded the family forceps from public gaze. His career was marked with highs and lows, from acting as physician to King Charles II in 1673 to being hounded out of the country for practising without a licence.

It was only a question of time before other doctors developed their own forceps. Among them was William Smellie (1697–1763), a pioneer obstetrician known for treating the poor and having genuine concern for newborns. He introduced refinements to the Chamberlens' design. His blades were covered in leather and lubricated with lard for comfort and cleanliness. His design also accommodated the curve of a woman's pelvis, and could be inserted a blade at a time.

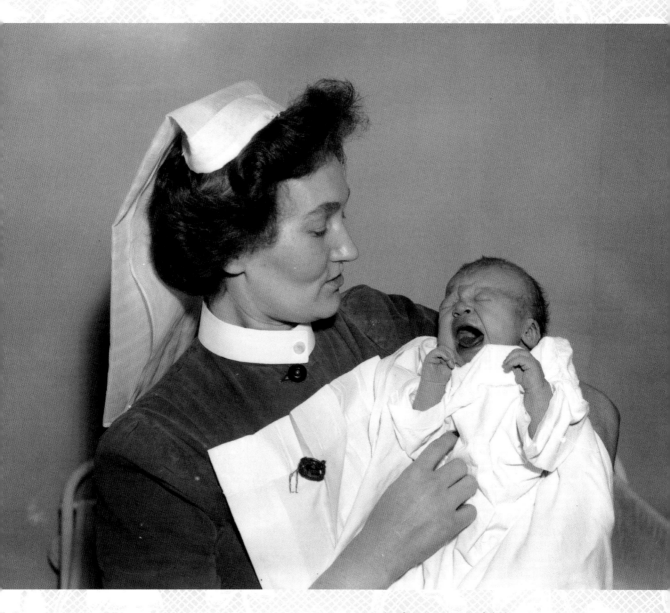

As Poplar mums turned their backs on home births, more children were born in East London Maternity Hospital than ever before, including baby McDonald in 1957, here being held by staff member Dorothy Vinall.

FORCEPS

FEELING RATHER PLEASED WITH MYSELF. I performed a textbook forceps delivery this evening on a patient with a deep transverse arrest. I rewarded myself with a late whisky and tried to imagine the look on old Dudley-Fisher's face!

I was not the most promising medical student, yet Dudley-Fisher could make the teaching of obstetrics feel more like square bashing. 'They're forceps, Turner! You're delivering a baby, not trying to crack a nut!'

I got the hang of it in the end. Despite the mystique, there's something rather ancient and crude about forceps. A tool of necessity, reduced to its plainest function: to grab and pull new life into the world. The design has hardly changed in centuries.

The story goes that modern forceps were invented by a family of Huguenots in the sixteenth century. They were said to have guarded their invention jealously - chasing others from the room before use, and even blindfolding the mother, lest she should betray the design to rivals! I rather think a mother has more pressing matters on her mind than commercial espionage.

Thankfully the secret got out - although perhaps an unnecessary

'They're forceps, Turner! You're delivering a baby, not trying to crack a nut!'

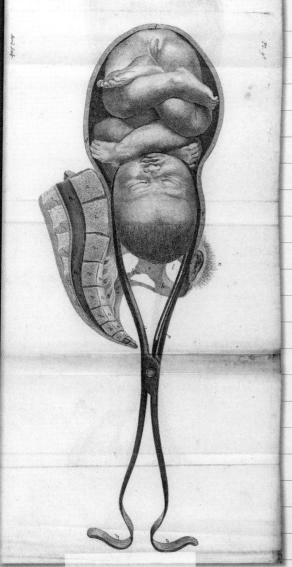

exclusivity remains. Midwives are not permitted to use forceps themselves, and so I must be summoned whenever complications arise. Mrs Ward's baby had failed to rotate its head into the correct position for birth, and so forceps were needed for manipulation and extraction. The blades are placed separately into position around the infant's skull before the apparatus is fastened together. Then, with the mother's help, the child can be both pushed and pulled to safety.

There is, despite the instruments and expertise, a sense of shared endeavour in these moments. A sense that all participants – mother, midwife, doctor – are equal servants to the infant; separate elements of care that fasten themselves together in the final moment to drag a new life into being.

Separate blades in the single ancient apparatus of humanity.

t was a skilful business, to extract a baby with the clunky tool without causing it death or injury.

Perhaps that's why there was a growing trend after Smellie's death to forgo the use of forceps. However, that fashion came to a dramatic end with the death of Princess Charlotte, the daughter of King George IV, in 1817 following a fifty-hour labour. Her baby was stillborn while she suffered a fatal haemorrhage. The event was particularly significant because it left the king without an heir. Royal physician Sir Richard Croft was so acutely aware of the uncomfortable dilemma that he shot himself with two pistols, one on each side of his head. In fact, the death of Princess Charlotte ultimately led to the accession of Queen Victoria, who reigned over one of the most dynamic eras in British history.

Croft's successor, David Davis, went on to develop more forceps designs with the safety of both mother and baby in mind. Since then the design has been modified many times. Success with forceps improved once medics could accurately assess the position of the unborn baby and could even safely turn its head before liberating it from the womb. But despite improvements, forceps were never ideal when the baby was lodged high in a woman's pelvis.

For this reason Caesarean sections evolved, finally becoming a more popular choice in twenty-first-century childbirth than forceps. It was long held that Roman leader Julius Caesar (100–44 BC) was born by Caesarean section, hence the name given to the operation. However, an operation like that during the Roman era – and for centuries afterwards – would have been fatal to a mother, and his is known to have lived to see her son's success.

There were occasions down the centuries when babies were ripped from the wombs of their mothers, if the woman giving birth was dying or dead. There's also said to be a case dating from the 1580s in which the woman survived. The operation was carried out in a Swiss village by her husband, a pig man. It sounds unfeasible, but during that same era a school for midwives was established in Paris, so a few fundamentals must have been known.

However, it wasn't until medical research carried out on dead bodies helped doctors understand what occurred during childbirth, coupled with the arrival of anaesthetics like chloroform, that Caesareans could be performed with any confidence. In Ireland, midwife Mary Donally performed a first Caesarian in 1738, while in England Dr James Barlow did the same in 1793. Perhaps curiously, the first to happen in South Africa outside the sphere of indigenous healers was performed in 1821 by a woman masquerading as a man. James Miranda Barry joined the military after graduating from Edinburgh, successfully hiding her sexuality until her death in 1865.

In Ireland alone a barbaric procedure called symphysiotomy was used in place of Caesareans. An estimated 1,500 women underwent this eighteenth-century birthing practice – which involved sawing through the pelvic cartilege or bone – between 1944 and 1983. It was favoured by a few hospitals on religious grounds in preference to Caesareans, the numbers of which were limited to three or four. After that, it was feared a woman would resort

It was a skilful business, to extract a baby with the clunky tool without causing it death or injury.

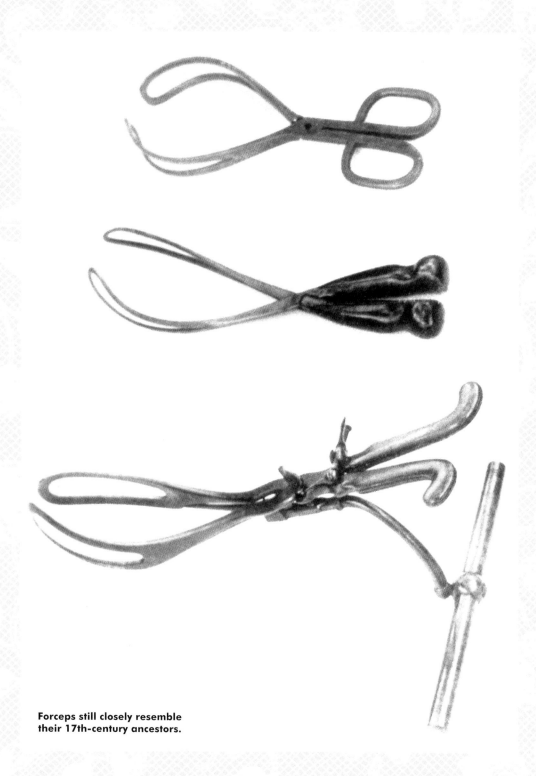

Forceps still closely resemble their 17th-century ancestors.

There had been significant successes in cutting the child mortality rate throughout the twentieth century. In 1900 there were 170 deaths for every thousand live births. By 1948 that figure had fallen to thirty-five, and the number of women who died in childbirth was falling, too.

there were 170 deaths for every thousand live births. By 1948 that figure had fallen to thirty-five, and the number of women who died in childbirth was falling, too.

One report published as early as 1953 claimed that the chief factor in these dramatic falls was down to superior hospital staffing; this was perhaps an early indicator of government thinking. It is doubtful that hospitals were statistically significant at the time, as many women were still having their babies at home without considering an alternative. In truth there were numerous social and economic reasons that contributed to the change, with housing, hygiene and nutrition better than ever before. Drug therapies used by hospitals and GPs at home births, notably the sulphonamides, made a vast difference after they came into use from 1936. But some pregnancies were still destined to end in sorrow, with women going home to silent cots and empty prams.

Stillbirths were for centuries never willingly disclosed or discussed. There was nothing that medical progress could do to aid the baby, and no importance was attached to the emotional issues bequeathed to the mother. Any genetic reason behind a stillbirth was unknown.

For premature babies there was some

to birth control so that's why they were sidestepped. Unsurprisingly, the women – who didn't give their permission for the operation – were often left in agony for years afterwards.

The ongoing battle against bacteria also yielded results that directly affected the survival chances of a woman undergoing the Caesarean operation. From 1906 a low incision was made in preference to one in the upper part of the uterus, where the wound healed more slowly.

Forceps are still used today, but they are considered in the same bracket as stirrups – something mostly associated with the past. Caesareans, on the other hand, are being employed more than ever, despite the lengthy recovery times for young mums. Just 4.5 per cent of births in 1970 were by Caesarean, while the figure in 2005 was approaching a quarter. Fear of litigation, a rise in obesity with its associated problems, difficulties detected in unborn babies and demand from women are among the reasons for this.

Thus there had been significant successes in cutting the child mortality rate throughout the twentieth century. In 1900

Stillbirths were for centuries never willingly disclosed or discussed. There was nothing that medical progress could do to aid the baby, and no importance was attached to the emotional issues bequeathed to the mother.

The warmth and protection afforded by even the most rudimentary incubators helped premature babies to survive.

hope. In 1880 incubators first appeared in France in a bid to save young lives that hung precariously in the balance. The idea came from chicken hatcheries; the incubators provided warmth and some degree of protection for early arrivals. Not everyone was convinced that this was the solution, however. Adolphe Pinard (1844–1934), a French obstetrician who invented a stethoscope to detect foetal heartbeats, advocated maternity leave and extra support for poor, malnourished women prior to giving birth to reduce the numbers of premature babies.

There was a body of opinion which said that premature babies were likely to die in later infancy, no matter what

early efforts were made on their behalf. For their part, mothers were not keen on incubators, as they didn't want to be parted from babies they could tend to themselves, and feared compromising hygiene. Nonetheless, incubators were used around the Western world after being memorably showcased at the Berlin Exposition in 1896. And just as premature births have led to grief, so there have been stories of triumph. Scientist Sir Isaac Newton, wartime premier Sir Winston Churchill, ballerina Anna Pavlova and writer Mark Twain were all reputedly premature.

There were exceptions, but in the sixties newborns were not considered viable until thirty-four weeks.

PREMATURE BIRTHS

A MUCH-LOVED WAY TO DESCRIBE A MOTHER EXPECTING A CHILD IS TO SAY THAT SHE HAS A 'BUN IN THE OVEN'. Less well known is the fact that one child in every baker's dozen will come out before it's fully baked. Premature birth can be a stressful business - but thankfully it's become an event that's far less tinged with tragedy.

Colette Wimbish, one of my mothers, knows all about that. She's had three pregnancies that have ended prematurely, and all without a happy ending. It's not surprising she's been nervous about her latest.

A premature birth is one that occurs before the thirty-seventh week. The earlier it happens, the more problems an infant can face. The respiratory system may not be fully formed, so breathing can be a problem; the child lacks the body fat to regulate its temperature, so may quickly develop hypothermia; there can be problems with digestion and a heightened susceptibility to infection. Such a child must be given the very highest care we can provide - and very quickly.

Mrs Wimbish turned up at the surgery with contractions at thirty-three weeks, so I gave her a bed at the maternity home to keep an eye on things. I'm glad I did. Her waters broke the next day, and we were off.

Things moved very quickly. The Obstetric Flying Squad were called, but before they'd arrived her daughter was born. Our relief was curtailed by the silence that followed. She wasn't breathing. I extracted the mucus from her airways and we tried our best to rub some warmth into her.

Then her cry. That most wonderful of things. A victorious will to live.

I'd barely had time to show baby to mother when the squad arrived with their equipment. The portable incubator and breathing apparatus were deployed, and in an instant the tiny thing was gone - temporary ward of a health-care system that has risen to meet ancient challenges with new speed. She was whisked away to be incubated and sustained until she was fit to face the world she'd entered in such haste.

There's a fine umbilical cord that now connects the weakest of our kind with the strongest care available. A human cord - the doctors, nurses, ambulance staff, surgeons, pharmacists and scientists who work tirelessly to serve the spirit of Hippocrates: dedicated to the preservation of health without discrimination, and to the maximum extent of its powers.

Colette was understandably bereft. You can emphasise the necessity of this separation, yet a mother's bond with her child is older and deeper than any logical argument medicine can muster. I hope it's not too long before they're reunited, and those ghosts of her past can finally be eased by the new life in her arms.

LOVE, FULLY BAKED.

**Dr Turner and Shelagh try
to reassure an anxious
Colette Wimbish.**

f privation during pregnancy scaled up the risk of premature birth, then mums in Poplar were still at risk even as other parts of the country were defeating environmental hardships.

Despite improvements in living standards – including the arrival of numerous prefabs that remained in Poplar until 1958 – and the mighty efforts of indomitable housewives, there was still a level of grime not common in homes today. In the worst cases a number of homes without bathrooms shared a single toilet. Midwives frequently used bars of soap to catch fleas, and stood bed legs in bottle lids filled with water to halt the progress of cockroaches. Bed bugs were legion, as were rodent infestations.

In most homes health standards were compromised; for example, there were no refrigerators or automatic washing machines. In the absence of a television set, children played in the street, improvising with the unwashed objects they found around them. Men would often sit on well-shined doorsteps playing dominoes.

Nationally, those who aspired to be more middle class often eschewed breastfeeding in favour of the bottle, in response to the glossy advertisements for formula that were appearing in magazines. However, few women had the capacity to properly sterilise equipment and were often tempted to dilute quantities to make the powder go further. This increased the risk of gastroenteritis among babies.

Earlier still some women had begun feeding their babies with milk from animals, especially cows. This was often modified with sugar, honey and so on. Before the nineteenth century ended, condensed milk, with its long shelf life, was used for babies – despite doctors' concerns about the high sugar levels.

From the twenties onwards there was evaporated milk, which also had a long shelf-life and enhanced sugar levels. Fortunately babies survived, despite their surroundings, to be called modern names like Michael, James, David, Robert and John. Among the least popular names were Frederick and Harry. Girls were most likely to be called Mary, Susan, Linda, Debra and Karen.

If privation during pregnancy scaled up the risk of premature birth, then mums in Poplar were still at risk even as other parts of the country were defeating environmental hardships.

STILLBIRTH

TODAY I ATTENDED A MOVING SERVICE AT NONNATUS HOUSE.
It was conducted by the Reverend Tom Hereward on behalf of Abigail and
Terence Bissette, two patients of mine. It was a service of remembrance
for their stillborn daughter, April. No one who attended could fail to be
moved. There was dignity and grace, and new ritual for an ancient grief.

Stillbirth is a loss that cries to be heard. It visits one in every
two hundred births: a condition with many causes but with a singular,
bitter end. The months of hope and love and imagining of futures become
a confusion of pain and anguish that receives no reply.

I was called by Nurses Mount and Gilbert to attend the Bissette
home after the child was born. Pain hung over the room like fog.
Young midwives are rarely prepared for the impact of such an event.
Procedure was the crutch that held them up. Abigail was in acute pain,
and it looked like the placenta might be trapped in the cervix.

To my surprise it was an undiagnosed twin – alive and imminent.
Young Terence Junior was born soon after: a bright mercy to hang the
day upon.

I took the son to see his father. Terence held the child and dared
to believe in a careful kind of joy. Nearby, a tiny corpse lay wrapped
in towelling, limp and unmentioned.

The stillborn child is an orphan of both Church and State.
There are no established ceremonies, graveyard rites or public

*April's name was invoked in unique prayer:
her lost life acknowledged in ceremony.*

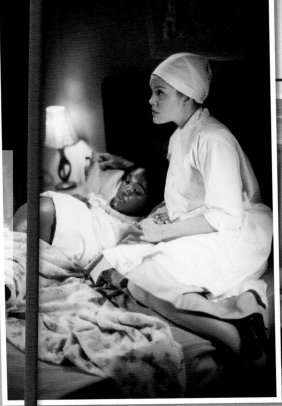

acknowledgements. There is only a mother's mute pain, and the embarrassed silence that greets her tears. The little body is removed with well-intentioned haste. Yet a mother will never hold it for herself - will never be granted the dignity to resolve the sorrow in her own arms.

Abigail's heart was not to be placated. She became depressed - and filled the hole left by the tragedy with self-blame. How could she bid farewell to a love she was not permitted to feel?

It was Reverend Hereward who found the means to answer. April's name was invoked in unique prayer: her lost life acknowledged in ceremony. She was made real by the will of those present. Love poured into the space left by her loss, and found a healing home. One did not need faith to see the therapeutic wisdom in the moment.

Remembrance is not a passive thing. It is a shouted testimony: an acknowledgement that love and loss are twin children to any life meaningfully lived - and both must be named.

Dr. Patrick Turner

| PHONE: POPLAR 491 | GMC No. 89502 | 19 KENILWORTH ROW, E14 |

FOR .... DATE ....

CHAPTER 5

The Shadow of Fear

19, KENILWORTH ROW
E14
POPLAR   LONDON ....

TUBERCULOSIS

IS IT MEANINGFUL TO HATE A BACTERIUM? In the same way you might detest somebody motivated by malice towards those you hold most dear?

I write this in a small roadside café, nursing a tea, and taking a breath on the drive back from the sanatorium. Poplar can wait. I need to order my thoughts.

There were few words. Sister Bernadette was grateful and polite, but insisted on entering the institution alone. She looked tiny in the doorway. Then she was gone - swallowed by the beast.

Mycobacterium tuberculosis. A scourge older than the pyramids. Known by many names, like some biblical demon. Consumption. TB. The White Plague. Contagious and patient, it spreads like fire through the coughs and sneezes of crowded humanity, yet it can hide away undetected for years. Scarring the lungs and stealing the breath. A taker of lives. A thief of time.

Hard to believe it's been little more than two weeks since our meeting with the Board of Health. It feels like a lifetime. So much gained. So much lost.

She was so wonderful that day. The mass X-ray programme was built for places like Poplar. I'd been promised a mobile X-ray van for the district months ago, yet heard nothing but excuses. I argued my case to the board and could feel my temper rising. I had three cases of TB in just one week! Our tenements are overcrowded - a breeding ground for epidemic. Early detection by X-ray is essential to isolate

those infected and protect the vulnerable. Sister Bernadette made a passionate case for the children's lives at stake if we delayed any longer.

This time they listened. Ten days later we had our van!

What a day. Patients crowding to the mobile X-ray unit to be screened. I couldn't have conjured a better vision for our Health Service than the queues I saw that day. We were smoking the old demon out from the lungs of our neighbourhood, patient by patient. With every X-ray we grew stronger. Kindness and compassion penetrating the skin. Sister Bernadette even demonstrated the machine for a frightened child, to show its harmlessness.

Rather a cruel touch, in retrospect. When her X-ray was processed, the lesions were unmistakable. I examined her myself. Her breathing crackled with infection. A demon's malice.

We've come on so much in the treatment of tuberculosis. The new 'triple treatment' of drugs combined with isolation and rest can work miracles. It need not mean the end.

My tea has grown cold from neglect. The old waitress is coughing as she cleans around my feet. I find myself listening to the sound of her constricted breath as it wheezes and crackles, wary of what can lie hidden to swallow us.

t was a name that once inspired cold fear whenever it was mentioned. Perhaps that's why tuberculosis has been given alternative monikers over time – consumption, phthisis, the Captain of Death and the White Plague.

Tuberculosis was something of an A-lister among diseases. With luminaries such as the poet John Keats (1795–1821), composer Frédéric Chopin (1810–1849), playwright Anton Chekhov (1860–1904), author Franz Kafka (1883–1924) and writer George Orwell (1903–1950) falling victim to it, an association between TB and the doomed creative soul was forged in public perception. Thus it became a melancholy malady depicted by romantics in art, literature and music.

In fact there was nothing tender or glamorous about this dreadful disease, which was responsible for killing one in four people in Britain in the eighteenth century, with its spread reaching epidemic proportions following the Industrial Revolution.

Although it did not respect social boundaries and undoubtedly did claim the lives of many rich and famous people,

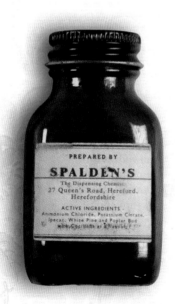

PREPARED BY
SPALDEN'S
The Dispensing Chemist
27 Queen's Road, Hereford,
Herefordshire

ACTIVE INGREDIENTS
Ammonium Chloride, Potassium Citrate,
Ipecac, White Pine and Poplar Bud

TB was at its most deadly when it came to poor communities, with those who lived at close quarters with others most at risk. It was spread by coughs and sneezes, but spitting in the street and other unwholesome habits did nothing to contain an outbreak.

Recent scientific research has proved that TB was present in the bodies of prehistoric men, although that's not to say they died because of it. Tuberculosis can exist in a latent form, causing no problems at all for its otherwise healthy host. However, if it awoke to ravage its victim, they were racked with a hacking cough, frequently bringing up blood. Feverish and fatigued, they were also disabled by pain in whichever part of their body harboured the disease. Tuberculosis mostly affects the lungs, which are the first place it settles after being inhaled, but it can manifest itself elsewhere, too, including in the bones and the brain. Death either came quickly, thanks to what was dubbed 'galloping consumption', or it might take years.

From the eighteenth century it was freely exported around the world by Westerners, as little was known about how it was transmitted. Mystery surrounded the illness until 1882, when German doctor Robert Koch (1843–1910) revealed in a lecture to the Berlin Physiological Society that TB was caused by a bacterium.

On that night he said: 'If the importance of a disease for mankind is measured by the number of fatalities it

TB was at its most deadly when it came to poor communities, with those who lived at close quarters with others most at risk.

Even after Robert Koch identified the bacteria that caused tuberculosis, it was years before a cure was found.

'If the importance of a disease for mankind is measured by the number of fatalities it causes, then tuberculosis must be considered much more important than those most-feared infectious diseases – plague, cholera and the like. One in seven of all human beings dies from tuberculosis.'

ROBERT KOCH

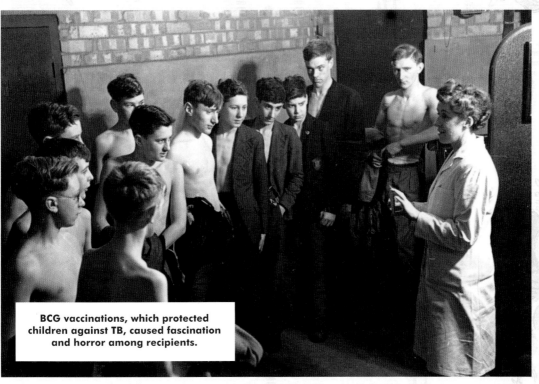

BCG vaccinations, which protected children against TB, caused fascination and horror among recipients.

DO NOT SPIT

WITHOUT REMEMBERING THAT TUBERCULOSIS IS SPREAD BY THIS MEANS

After Koch declared that a bacteria caused TB there was a better understanding about how to prevent its spread. This poster dating from 1910 urges people to improve their personal habits to help curb the disease.

ISSUED BY
NATIONAL ASSOCIATION FOR THE PREVENTION OF TUBERCULOSIS.
1 GORDON SQUARE, LONDON, W.C.1.

The government asked people to consider the regular use of hand-kerchiefs as a matter of public health. With city streets more populated than ever, an unfettered sneeze by an infectious person could have dire consequences.

causes, then TB must be considered much more important than those most-feared infectious diseases – plague, cholera and the like. One in seven of all human beings dies from tuberculosis.'

To illustrate his methodology, Koch took with him the contents of a laboratory so he could share what he'd found. Step by step he showed how a single bacterium was affecting apes, the brains and lungs of humans and the stomachs of cows. Rather than bearing numerous different names, the disease could now be known by one. Accordingly, he officially introduced the rod-shaped, waxy-coated *Mycobacterium tuberculosis* to the assembled crowd. When his lecture finished there was silence, as the enormity of his findings slowly sank in. One scientist, Paul Ehrlich, dubbed it 'the most important experience of my scientific life'.

Koch had previously worked with anthrax, and went on to examine cholera. As a consequence, he became known as 'the father of bacteriology' and was presented with the Nobel Prize in Physiology or Medicine in 1905 'for his investigations and discoveries in relation to tuberculosis'.

> A long-running public health campaign run by the government throughout the forties about the perils of coughs and sneezes helped to elevate people's awareness, but it also instigated dread.

Others built on the platform of his findings – as he had done with other scientists' research before making his own breakthrough – and the fight against TB was conclusively under way. Yet even though much more was now known about TB, there was still little available by way of a cure. Koch went on to develop something he called tuberculin, but his hopes that it would kill off the disease were soon dashed.

In 1895 the arrival of X-ray machines helped immeasurably in diagnosis, as did a skin test developed using Koch's tuberculin that revealed the possible presence of the disease. The Mantoux test was developed in 1907 and hasn't been bettered. During the test a nurse injected a small amount of fluid containing tuberculin under the skin on a forearm. A few days later the site of the injection was examined to see if there had been a reaction. A response of redness and a small bump might indicate the presence of TB, and the patient would be sent for chest X-rays and a test of sputum samples. The same test is still in use today.

More significantly, a vaccine was developed by Albert Calmette (1863–1933)

Dr. Williams' Pink Pills break a Record.

"I was discharged, incurable, with Tuberculosis, from the Tavistock Cottage Hospital. I took Dr. Williams' Pink Pills—five boxes altogether, and kept gaining strength. I am now perfectly well—and that was ten months ago."

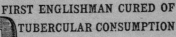

FIRST ENGLISHMAN CURED OF TUBERCULAR CONSUMPTION

CHENHALL & SON,
Tavistock.

Portrait of Mr. J. G. ROGERS.

THE following case is remarkable, as Mr. Rogers is the first man in England to be cured of tubercular consumption—hitherto regarded, even by Dr. Williams, as incurable. The other form of consumption (marked by blood-spitting and night-sweats) has many times been cured by Dr. Williams' Pink Pills.

Mr. Rogers' statement is transcribed from the newspaper which had the honour of being the first to announce this modern medical miracle—the *Tavistock Gazette.*

"My name is John Giles Rogers, and I am a monumental mason. I was taken seriously ill at the age of twenty-four. A diseased bone in the foot was the first sign of my affliction, which was general tuberculosis. I went to the South Devon and East Cornwall Hospital, Plymouth, where I remained under treatment for six weeks. At the end of the six weeks I came out of the hospital, although my foot was not thoroughly healed. I went to work, and continued at my avocation by dint of great effort for three months. In the meantime I had been gradually losing flesh, my appetite was gone, I grew weaker every day, and at last was confined to my bed, suffering from general and increasing debility. There I remained for seven weeks, and then I was admitted to the Tavistock Cottage Hospital, where I stayed for three months. Every effort was made to improve my health but without avail, and I was discharged as incurable, with tuberculosis.

Mr. Rogers is now working at his trade.

"My friends were informed that nothing more could be done for me, and that I had not long to live. I had a severe pain in the back, was short of breath and could only crawl along. I never expected to go to work again, and everyone knew that I had the fatal tubercular form of consumption. The weakness of the spine and general debility increased to such an extent that I had to remain in bed again, and this time I thought that it was all up.

"One day, while glancing at the paper in bed, I read of a case of consumption cured by Dr. Williams' Pink Pills. I obtained a box of the pills, and took one after each principal meal—three a day—and after five days I was able to get out of bed. The pills produced an invigorating effect, and thoroughly braced me up.

"Two days later I was walking about the town. I took five boxes of Dr. Williams' Pink Pills altogether, and kept gaining strength. That was ten months ago. Since then I have never lost an hour but have regularly worked from 7 a.m. to 6 p.m.—ten hours a day. I have a good appetite, and am perfectly well."

The importance of this case is proportioned to the formerly fatal character of Tuberculosis, and to its prevalence. It is estimated that one seventh of the human race have died of this disease.

On the opposite page will be found a case of ordinary pulmonary consumption cured by Dr. Williams' Pink Pills.

---

and Camille Guérin (1872–1961) in France during the first two decades of the twentieth century. Known as the BCG, it was administered from 1921. However, disaster struck in Germany in 1927 when children were mistakenly injected with a live strain of TB, resulting in nearly 100 deaths. In any event, the BCG was not the silver bullet that many had hoped. It did provide protection, particularly for children, but was never found to provide blanket coverage.

Surgeons experimented with collapsing sufferers' lungs so that the affected lesions would heal. It was also thought such action would stop the spread of infection. But a truly effective treatment eluded medics. Thus there were few options for sufferers prior to the twentieth century.

From the 1800s a number of sanatoria were established, as doctors hoped that a regime of fresh air and rest would provide a remedy. For those with a slight affliction there may have been some benefit, but most who went still died. The sanatoria were an improvement on the notion of 'TB colonies', however, which had been mooted to 'cleanse' society of the disease's scourge. The wealthy went to luxury private venues, but the 41 public sanatoria in operation by

A Consumptive Girl Saved.

Treated by no less than thirteen doctors, Miss Stevens was "given up" as consumptive. Dr. Williams' Pink Pills entirely cured her, and have, without doubt, saved her life.

VICTOR HUBERT,
Tunbridge Wells

Portrait of MISS LEAH STEVENS.
(Present day.)

EVIDENCE OF TWO PHOTOGRAPHS.

CONSUMPTION is often thought incurable. There is a stage when no doubt the desease may go too far for treatment, but that is not to say that it is incurable at every stage; nor is every case pronounced by doctors incurable with ordinary medicine beyond hope, if Dr. Williams' Pink Pills for Pale People, which are *not* ordinary medicine, are used. They have cured many cases by replacing the lost blood, and increasing the resistant power of the lungs, whereby the patient is enabled to rally from the weakness the disease causes and eventually to throw it off. The first sign of cure is usually the cessation of the distressing night-sweats. Then the cough ceases and the patient begins to put on flesh. At Withyham, near Tunbridge Wells, a representative of the local paper, *Tunbridge Wells Advertiser*, hit upon an example. In a bailiff's cottage on the Buckhurst Park Estate, near the residence of Earl de la Warr, a lady exhibited with pardonable pride two photographs of her daughter, which bore but the faintest resemblance to one another. "This one," she said, "was taken two or three years ago"—producing a likeness in which the features portrayed were those of a consumptive but, withal, attractive-looking girl—"and this one"—producing a cabinet photo of the young lady, in which every sign of that consumption was effaced—"was taken a month or two ago."

The young lady herself said: "My name is Leah Stevens, and I have lived in this park nearly the whole of my life. My father died of consumption before I was a year old, and as I grew up such a puny child my friends thought that I also would die of the same disease.

Portrait of
MISS LEAH STEVENS.
(From a Photo. taken three years ago, while suffering from Consumption.)

I have been treated by no less than thirteen doctors. When I was twelve years old I was consumptive, and, as the treatment which I received appeared to do me no good, it was fully expected that I should follow my father before long. For two years I had to be carried up and down stairs, as the exertion was too much for me. When I was nineteen—after seven years in a consumption—we read of a similar case to mine having been cured by Dr. Williams' Pink Pills, and mother obtained some for me. I began taking them, and on the third day I felt so much better that I could enjoy my meals. At the end of a fortnight they told me that they could see the pink coming into my face, and my hopes began to rise. At the end of the month I walked four miles to chapel and home, unassisted. Altogether I took seven boxes of the pills, and from the time I ceased to take them, about eight months ago, until now, I have not had an hour's illness."

Consumption.

A wasting disease of the lungs. The patient is thin, or losing weight; spits blood; is weak, languid, and pale; has slight feverishness, shortness of breath, pain in the chest, and profuse perspiration, especially at night. This disease, incurable by ordinary medicine, has been frequently cured by Dr. Williams' Pink Pills, when taken in time. Consumption, if neglected or treated by ordinary medicine, invariably causes death.

In the 19th century, 'Pink Pills for Pale People' were sold to cure TB, rickets, flu, anaemia and a host of other ills, a quack remedy capitalising on the fears of desperate people.

1910 in Britain owed more to the workhouse than any health establishment. Patients had to work for bed and board despite illness. Nor could they expect much sympathy.

Despite the feted elite who had suffered from TB, there was a vicious backlash in the twentieth century against victims – a hangover from Victorian beliefs about 'the undeserving poor'. In 1912 Dr H. de Carle Woodcock, a member of the National Association for the Prevention of Tuberculosis, declared that 'sexual vice', 'alcoholic habits' and 'moral dirt' were the general characteristics of those who became ill. 'The beautiful and the rich receive it from the unbeautiful poor,' he explained.

Despite Koch's findings, it was still widely believed that TB was hereditary, and perhaps that's why Woodcock thought as he did. To further compound this view Dr Leonard Hill, from the National Institute for Medical Research, said in 1935: 'Consumptives, in their own interests but particularly in the interests of the nation, should be sterilised.'

All this served to foster a burning shame among those who were unfortunate enough to contract the illness. If they made a recovery, they were frequently snubbed when they returned from the sanatorium to society at large. Afterwards TB became a mental issue as well as a physical one. People were reluctant to even be in the proximity of chest clinics, for fear of being stigmatised by the disease. There was a keenness among health authorities to keep infectious diseases like TB away from general hospitals, too.

People with TB were often evicted from their homes by fearful landlords. Once they had gone, the premises and items inside were routinely sterilised to kill off rogue bacteria. In 1959 more than seventy places in Poplar were disinfected by the local authority on account of TB, along with 559 different items.

Anyone who had been in contact with someone diagnosed with TB was tracked down and notified, in much the same way that contacts with Ebola victims are traced today. However, 'drifters' who went between districts without seeking proper medical help were continuing to spread the disease. A long-running public health campaign run by the government throughout the forties about the perils of coughs and sneezes helped to elevate people's awareness, but it also instigated dread.

Tuberculosis was also spread in milk, yet opinion was divided throughout the thirties and forties about whether

People with TB were often evicted from their homes by fearful landlords. Once they had gone, the premises and items inside were routinely sterilised to kill off rogue bacteria.

milk should be pasteurised. There was talk that the process would affect its nutritional value or flavour. But, as things stood, a cowman suffering with TB in the Cotswolds could infect vast swathes of London. It was the same story if there was a single infected cow in a herd.

A report published in the *British Medical Journal* in 1943 was blunt. 'Objections are frequently raised ... on pseudo-scientific grounds but the real objection in the past has been financial and has come from the producer-retailers.' The report, by G.S. Wilson, Professor of Bacteriology at the London School of Hygiene and Tropical Medicine, acknowledged milk as 'a food of exceptional value for a growing child' but warned that up to 10 per cent of the country's farms were sending out milk which contained the bacillus that caused TB.

There were other health risks associated with milk at the time, linked to diphtheria, scarlet fever and typhoid. The relevant bacteria came either from the cow's udders, the infected hands of those handling the milk, from the coughs and sneezes of cowmen or from water used to clean the cows and equipment. Milk was used locally and shipped to large cities. If doctors had concerns after farmhands were diagnosed with TB, there seemed

Clearly, the Chief Medical Officer had some insight into the problem. There were nine deaths in the borough that year recorded as being caused by TB. By 1960 there were a total of 41 new cases discovered in Poplar alone, nearly a third of which were in those aged under 20. Chest clinics became focal points of the community for diagnosis, treatment and post-treatment check-ups. These figures must have been a matter of some disappointment, as one of the largest preventive programmes of vaccination had got under way among London schoolchildren in 1954, when they were given BCG jabs. Clearly, some had slipped through the net. To this day, TB has never been eradicated, although it no longer engenders panic when there are outbreaks. The fight against TB has had far-reaching effects, some of which are still in evidence.

In the 1870s, as America's new railways headed into previously uncharted territory, one slogan to tempt TB sufferers was 'Head west and have health'. Accordingly, major western cities were built including Tucson, Colorado Springs and Albuquerque. Cities such as Los Angeles were settled in great numbers by TB sufferers at the turn of the twentieth century, determined to reap the benefits of a sunny, dry climate.

Before Koch discovered that TB was spread by infection, ice cream had commonly been sold as a 'penny lick' in a glass container, to be re-used by subsequent customers. In London the glass containers were banned in 1899, while in America ice-cream vendors developed first pastry and then waffle cones to replace them. By 1924 cone production had reached 245 million. Hemlines went up and beards came off with the twin realisations that long skirts and facial hair could harbour germs. General personal hygiene, especially among children, improved; they were taught to wash their hands and clean their teeth regularly to evade disease.

Penny licks were popular until their role in the spread of TB was discovered. Eventually the ice cream cone replaced glass dishes that had been recycled among customers with only elementary hygiene in place.

Dr. Patrick Turner

PHONE: POPLAR 491 GMC No. 89502 19 KENILWORTH ROW, E14

FOR .... DATE ....

CHAPTER 6

Sheltering the Vulnerable

19, KENILWORTH ROW
E14
POPLAR LONDON ....

PRESCRIPTION No. ....

Although television was in its infancy in the fifties, it was already proving a potent tool for communicating matters of health, even if the number of homes with a TV was limited. *The Hurt Mind*, a series of five programmes addressing mental health issues, was broadcast in 1957. As it brought difficult topics right into the home, it was widely deemed controversial, even dangerous. However, William Sargant, medical adviser to *The Hurt Mind*, believed it could reach at least some of the 5,000 people who committed suicide each year.

In the same vein, on 11 February 1958 the BBC broadcast the first in a new eight-part series called *Your Life in Their Hands*, presented by Charles Fletcher of Hammersmith Hospital, who was intent on improving doctor–patient communication. Each programme dealt with a different topic, such as head injuries, the thyroid gland or radiotherapy for cancer sufferers. Patients were diagnosed and treated on camera. Fletcher was duly criticised by the *British Medical Journal*, which felt it was inappropriate for medical matters to masquerade as popular entertainment. The *BMJ* said: 'There can be no doubt of the danger to the unstable with a morbid curiosity about blood and bowels, to frail worriers, and to those with serious disease who may receive interpretations different from those given by their own doctors.'

There were also critics among the nation's politicians, at least one of whom asked the Attorney General to put a stop to the series, and condemnation focused on the filming of operations, which could, it was said, disturb the concentration of medical staff. Some doctors were also concerned that the mystique of medicine, something cherished by practitioners, was being eroded.

The programme inspired other problems, too, with some viewers fainting

Although television was in its infancy in the fifties, it was already proving a potent tool for communicating matters of health.

at home at the sight of an operation and suffering concussion, while others became neurotic. There were also complaints of intrusion, with an uneasy comparison being made with the bygone habit of visiting the deranged incarcerated at Bedlam hospital. However, the BBC fought hard against accusations of sensationalism, working in relative harmony with the hospitals it visited. In the programme's favour was the inspiration it provided for would-be nurses and the education of viewers about modern medicine.

In the programme's cross-hairs were doctors who were wedded to ideas of patriarchy that should have disappeared when then NHS was introduced, as there was a sense that some doctors – unlike Dr Turner – were dwelling in a backwater as far as treatments were concerned, at the expense of their patients.

After a three-year break the original series returned in 1961, ran regularly until 1964, and has been revived several times since then. Flickering in grey-green on the nation's tiny TV screens was the modern face of medicine; a revelation of what was going on at its cutting edge. What viewers saw must have amazed them, and public attitudes began to be transformed. Nowhere was this more important than in the arena of physical disability. There was a tendency for parents to hide children who had been born with disabilities from public view.

In 1964 the Spastics Society sought charitable donations to help children in its care. Although it now appears clumsily-named, the charity was a pace setter in a new age of giving that relied on cash from everyone when previously charity had been the domain of rich philanthropists.

JOHN IS A SPASTIC— he needs your help!

You'd love John. He's six years old and, like all small boys, mischief twinkles in his eyes. But John is a spastic. He desperately needs the care and training we can give him and thousands of children like him. Will you join us in getting John on his feet? Just put *whatever* you can spare in an envelope and post it to this address now: THE SPASTICS SOCIETY, 12 PARK CRESCENT, LONDON, W.1.

Looking back at the way things were, it's possible to appreciate the long journey that's been taken. For example, modern dictionaries define 'spastic' as a term of abuse. But during the era of *Call the Midwife* the word was commonly used to indicate anyone who had suffered brain damage at birth. According to a film narrated by Richard Dimbleby in 1960, there was a baby born every eight hours

who would fall into this bracket. There were, said Dimbleby, some 40,000 people with brain damage in Britain who were known – while others went under the radar after being hidden away by their families.

The film was made by The Spastics Society, which had been set up in the fifties by the parents of three children with cerebral palsy, with just £5. They had already been highly successful in raising a million pounds for treatments, schools and research, but there remained a cash shortfall when it came to realising their ambitions.

To raise money there were door-to-door collections, sticky Christmas seals, creative collecting boxes, piles of pennies in pubs and support from celebrities of the era, led by actor and broadcaster Wilfred Pickles.

There was a tendency for parents to hide children who had been born with disabilities from public view.

CARE OF THE DISABLED

WORDS CAN TOO EASILY BE AN INSTRUMENT OF EXCLUSION.
Words in medicine are like a cipher that confounds the uninitiated.
Words about one another are often like a wall that separates us from
the things we have in common.

'A defective.' That's what we call someone like Sally Harper.
PC Noakes recited the relevant clause of the Sexual Offences Act by way
of explanation. 'It is an offence to have unlawful sexual intercourse
with a defective.'

The term was meant to protect, not offend. It defined a blameless
broken thing that must be shielded from the wilful harm of others. Yet
in this terminology Sally was just an object: an indefinite article
used to blunt our own sharp discomfort at her inconvenient feelings.

The case of Sally Harper has given me a lot to reflect upon.
A young woman with Down's syndrome is not meant to fall pregnant -
particularly not in a reputable institution like St Gideon's. Such an
event is filled with hazards that the medical literature has signally
failed to address. How does one communicate the profound consequences
of labour to a mind made innocent by nature? Not only can an infant be
born premature, but it might also be more likely to suffer the mental
infirmities of the mother.

Sally had the full dignity of a midwife's care

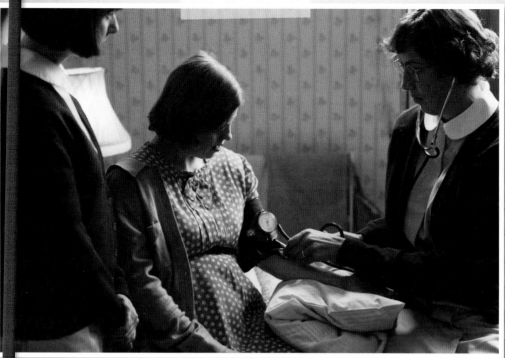

I was furious with St Gideon's - presuming the girl had been violated by a member of staff. My anger, like that of the police, had allowed me to overlook the possibility of consent. Yet when Jacob Milligan - a fellow St Gideon's resident - presented himself as the child's father, my righteousness was humbled. Jacob has profound physical impairment, but possesses a sharp mind and a clear sense of duty. He loved Miss Harper, and wanted to make her his wife. Moreover, Sally wanted the same. These so-called 'defectives' demonstrated a unity of human feeling as functional and sincere as any I had seen. My language had been inadequate, not theirs.

I resolved that Sally's labour should proceed as normally as possible, and avoid the involvement of the London at all costs. They would likely reduce her to a medical curiosity, rather than the young woman I now saw her to be.

Her labour was abrupt and premature. The child was stillborn and Sally was predictably distressed. Yet Nurses Noakes and Miller were at least able to supervise. Sally had the full dignity of a midwife's care.

I heard that Jacob was later sent north to a new institution. Painful, but inevitable. How could their relationship be permitted to succeed? Sally couldn't comprehend the responsibilities and burdens of human intercourse, as Jacob could. Yet why should their love require any more comprehension than their own?

Perhaps our society's lexicon can't permit words of human desire to exist between those we've declared mute and senseless. It would mean that those we exclude from the vocabulary of full humanity possess a language as full and as sensuous as our own - and what would that say about the rest of us?

Sally Harper shines at the
St Gideon's dance.

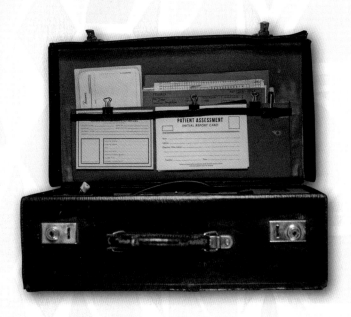

The word 'spastic' was derived from 'spasm', reflecting the fact that many people with brain damage cannot control minute movements. In 1994, with the word by now a well-established insult, the charity changed its name to Scope. Charities such as this one still play a significant role despite the existence of the NHS. In Victorian times charities had helped families that were struggling. But with the arrival of the NHS it was thought they would no longer be required, as the government would provide the necessary welfare assistance.

There was a greater awareness of poverty and its effects after many comfortably-off middle-class people across Britain had been confronted by the parlous physical condition of the country's poor when they had welcomed evacuees from inner-cities into their homes at the beginning of the Second World War. The skeletal forms of the children who arrived were often plagued with lice and scabies, and the youngsters exhibited troubling social behaviour including bed-wetting.

Ultimately, hopes that the government would solve all society's ills were misplaced. Many charities survived the seismic shift in social care, including Barnardos, which had opened its first home for boys in Stepney in 1870 and, later, one for girls in Barkingside. There were a series of apparent failures in the system highlighted during the sixties that also brought new voluntary groups into being, including the hospice movement spearheaded by Dame Cicely Saunders, various cancer charities – including Marie Curie Cancer Care – and the homeless charity Shelter. Other existing charities assumed new importance and sometimes depended on government money to establish services.

Most charities were domestic, but some looked overseas to answer the plight of the war-affected and hungry. Oxfam began during the Second World War, but was really getting into its stride by the sixties and received significant exposure when it was publicly supported by The Beatles in 1963. However, charities really came into their own when childbirth – at home or in hospital – yielded unhappy surprises.

SPINA BIFIDA

I HAD TO VISIT THE ROBERTS FAMILY TO EXAMINE THEIR NEW SON TODAY. Spina bifida. Rotten shock for Ruby. It looked like Nurse Lee wasn't too comfortable with it either. I expect she hasn't seen this before.

I've always liked Douglas and Ruby. I know their daughters well. Scratches, coughs and bumps, of course, but generally two very healthy girls. Their son is going to need a lot more care.

Spina bifida is a birth defect of the backbone in which the spine fails to fully close around the spinal cord. In severe cases, it can cause the fluid and cord to protrude through the infant's back. Immobility, bladder and bowel problems are routine, and the poor mite also has hydrocephalus, which may impair his learning abilities.

We're lucky to have the London on our doorstep. Their advances in this field are world-leading. He will have the best treatment available. Yet the long-term prognosis is difficult. He's unlikely to live to adulthood.

It's hard to see Ruby brought so low. One becomes accustomed to that confident smile of hers. It can be hard for the mother in such circumstances. Humans are driven to seek a cause for life's effects - and a mother's instinct can make her feel doubly responsible for her child's fragility.

I've been asked why we even try to save these children - who in earlier times were humanely put out of what was regarded as a certain misery. Yet I've never had any difficulty in answering. A life isn't measured by the limits of time, the perceptions of another's pain, or by any presumption of a heart's potential. The chance to live, and to love, is a gift that can't be idly traded. Such a life doesn't define itself in isolation, but is forged in the reflected light of the love that surrounds it.

Ruby will find that smile again - reflected in the unquestioning trust of the fragile life she holds, and in the love she will carry for both of them.

CYSTIC FIBROSIS

I'VE ALWAYS BEEN EXERCISED BY ISSUES OF INHERITANCE.
The facts of a life are not the ultimate qualities of it; things
assigned to us by nature are just the opening statements, and not the
argument's end. After all, even something written in stone can be
eroded away to nothing given time and a fair wind.

This week presented me with a medical mystery - one where my
assumptions were the biggest obstacle to progress. Merle and Billy
Vickers have two young sons: toddler Ian, and newborn Martin. Merle
was finding it hard to manage. Martin was crying constantly - he looked
underweight and permanently hungry. Ian displayed symptoms of a
serious chest infection.

Billy and Merle are a happy couple - bright and kind. Yet when
I visited, one could sense the tension in the place. Merle was
struggling to cope and poor Billy was trying his best to help her.
It was clear that Martin wasn't thriving. I placed him on formula,
took samples and put him under observation. Ian needed a course of
penicillin. Yet the overall impression was of a family weighed down by
a mother's depression. Such a condition can never be underestimated.
It can leech the happiness from the best and strongest home.

Test results on the children showed nothing untoward - yet a week
later the Vickers were insisting they be taken to hospital. Ian was
choking with congestion. Nurse Lee informed me that Billy's brother,
the children's uncle, had died of a chest infection as a child. It
seemed that this was adding to their anxiety - they were haunted by a
past misfortune. Yet sometimes truth can arrive by a circuitous path.

That night, Sister Monica Joan turned up at my door - soaking wet and
brandishing an antique medical tome. She claimed that the answer to the

Vickers' problems lay inside. She's vulnerable to episodes of wandering and confusion, so I drove her straight back to Nonnatus House. Yet something in her conviction made me curious. I later compared passages in her book with the latest studies into a condition called cystic fibrosis - a hereditary affliction of the lungs and digestive system.

The sister had been absolutely right. Billy Vickers' brother and children had been cursed with genes that congest the body and shorten life. By the time I knew the truth, little Martin had suffered a fit. Yet the beast was named - opening statements known. Modern medicine could now do much to relieve the worst. One day it may even lift the curse.

The final argument? That belongs to the Vickers family. Merle and Billy have two beautiful children - lives to be lived, and love to be shared. To live in hope is not a deluded thing. Hope is the sword love wields in the face of uncertainty. It reflects the quality of a life complete, and not the mere facts that constitute a body's physiology.

Hope is the fair wind that can blow all writing from the stone.

Jenny (Jessica Raine) weighs Merle's baby

THE NATIONAL CHILDBIRTH TRUST IS BORN

Just as women were flocking to hospitals to give birth, believing them to be the best place for mother and baby, there were voices of dissent. A relatively small but not inconsiderable number of people who felt that childbirth should be a natural rather than a medical matter began to make their opinions heard.

Strong opposition to universal hospital admittance for expectant mums came from one doctor in particular, who had worked in both Coventry and Cornwall. Dr C. Fordyce Turner admitted to being 'a common or garden GP, fond of domiciliary midwifery, with some 27 years' experience of a busy industrial practice and three years now of a truly rural small practice.' When he gave his views to the government as it was looking into maternity care, he

Long before childbirth comprehensively moved from the home to the hospital – and prior to the era of *Call the Midwife* – Grantly Dick-Read (1890–1959) had advocated a more natural method of childbirth.

admitted that his approach was more practical than scientific or academic.

He felt there was too much official and unofficial propaganda calculated to frighten pregnant women, and that duplication of paperwork between surgeries and hospitals was wasteful and inspired mistrust between the two branches of medicine. The advantages of home births, he said, were the presence of father and family at the birth, and an atmosphere of trust and confidence.

Speaking anecdotally in 1957, Doctor Fordyce Turner felt that infections were

Left: Grantly Dick-Read insisted women were never left alone in childbirth 'prey to the destructive forces of uncontrolled imagination' which, he believed, caused pain.

Opposite: Appalled by a hospital stay, Prunella Briance was inspired by Dick-Read's teachings and formed a natural childbirth group.

more prevalent in hospitals. 'I was not so impressed by the standard of hospital in-patient nursing, especially as evidenced by the rate of both breastfeeding and minor infections.

'My mind goes back to one or two of the old "private" midwives, who may have been old-fashioned in their methods and imperfect in asepsis [hygiene] but whose personal knowledge of their patients and enduring interest in the children was truly remarkable.

'The younger GPs showed a high standard of technical knowledge, but with the advent of the NHS there developed a strong tendency to book cases without any apparent intention to attend in labour and a lack of enthusiasm for what might be called the human angle of midwifery.'

Long before childbirth comprehensively moved from the home to the hospital – and prior to the era of *Call the Midwife* – Grantly Dick-Read (1890–1959) had advocated a more natural method of childbirth.

An obstetrician who qualified at the London Hospital in 1914, his books – *Natural Childbirth*, published in 1933 and *Childbirth without Fear*, published in 1942 – expounded his belief in non-intervention. Indeed, he believed that interference was a major cause of infant and maternal deaths. He said: '[The clinician] should use the method that gives the best and safest result from all points of view until something better is discovered.'

It was Dick-Read's theories that inspired Prunella Briance to form a group for mothers who wanted a different kind of birth from the one most commonly experienced. Briance had had a stillborn

daughter at a London hospital and believed that medical intervention was to blame for the tragedy. In 1956 she placed an advertisement and box number in *The Times*, saying 'A Natural Childbirth Association is to be formed for the promotion and better understanding of the Dick-Read system.'

The association's inaugural meeting was the following year, with Dick-Read appearing as a speaker. The NCA became the Natural Childbirth Trust in 1958, with its first antenatal class being held a year later. By 1960 the NCT was lobbying the government about the overuse of intervention during childbirth. It was renamed for a final time as the National Childbirth Trust in 1961, the same year it won charitable status.

Briance was not alone in her concerns about the way childbirth was being centred in hospitals and medicalised, to the detriment of women. American author and poet Sylvia Plath had the heroine of her book *The Bell Jar*, published in 1963, reeling after seeing a woman in labour, so heavily drugged that any memory of the experience would be a blur.

'I thought it sounded just like the sort of drug a man would invent [...] she would go straight home and start another baby, because the drug would make her forget how bad the pain had been, when all the time, in some secret part of her, that long, blind, doorless and windowless corridor of pain was waiting to open up and shut her in again.'

Also in America – where women were sometimes tied to a gurney during labour – Elisabeth Bing was promoting the theories of Dick-Read. Then she encountered the work of Dr Fernand Lamaze (1891–1957), a French doctor who encountered new methods of childbirth in Russia when he visited in 1951. Under his guidance, drugs were banished in favour of childbirth classes that taught relaxation, massage and breathing techniques, and encouraged emotional support from husbands. This birth philosophy became known as the Lamaze method. The theories underpinning the Lamaze method were that women should move freely during a labour that began naturally, with the threat of intervention removed. From 1960 a not-for-profit organisation began in America to spread the message about Lamaze.

There were also those who disliked hospitals not for their methods or the use of pain-relief, but for a fundamental lack of compassion towards new mums. Back in Britain in the same year a letter appeared in the *Observer* from a Sally Willington, telling how mothers put up with 'loneliness, lack of sympathy, lack of privacy, lack of consideration, poor food, unlikely visiting hours, callousness, regimentation, a complete disregard for mental care or the personality of the mother'.

The result of this movement was the formation of the Society for the Prevention of Cruelty to Pregnant Women, swiftly renamed the Association for Improvements in the Maternity Services (AIMS). Its initial emphasis was on better care for women in hospital, which meant tackling the regimentation inflicted on patients by staff, and toning down the levels of deference medics had come to expect. One outcome was the admission of fathers on to the labour ward, as a matter of course.

In 1966 Sir Robert Platt also lamented the lack of 'people skills' among recruits when he gave evidence to the Royal Commission on Medical Education about new doctors. 'Is it likely that the qualities required by a good doctor will be found

'I thought it sounded just like the sort of drug a man would invent [...] she would go straight home and start another baby, because the drug would make her forget how bad the pain had been, when all the time, in some secret part of her, that long, blind, doorless and windowless corridor of pain was waiting to open up and shut her in again.'
FROM SYLVIA PLATH'S *THE BELL JAR*, 1963

only in schoolboys and girls who have elected to specialise in science?' he asked. 'The few who would enter medicine from humane studies are at once penalised by an extra year of what to them may be drudgery at one of the most exciting times of their lives ... I would like to see at least one or two good medical schools encouraged to open their doors to any student who had shown himself to be of the intellectual calibre to take a good university degree. All my life I have been more interested in people and in the practice of medicine than in the laboratory. I cannot believe I am the only doctor who feels that way.'

Some innovations of the era slipped in quietly, such as co-operation cards for pregnant women, which arrived in the time of *Call the Midwife*. At last information on a woman's pregnancy was stored in one place and was available to doctors, midwives, health visitors and hospital consultants.

In its first newletter, AIMS called for protest among new mums who suffered indignities during a hospital birth.

Association for Improvements in the Maternity Services (AIMS).
(Society for the Prevention of Cruelty to Pregnant Women 1960)

Mrs. S. Willington, 1 Batchwood Gardens, St. Albans
HERTFORDSHIRE

A I M S - Newsletter 1.

Dear

The response has been good and the number of members is
now (   ) and they are from all over Britain - we have midwives,
doctors and obstetricians, wives and mothers, and enquiries from
matrons, newspapers and other organisations.

Some suspcious people want to know whom I am.   I am 28 and
have a girl of 3 and a boy of 1½.   I am a potter married to a
teacher.

The usual obstacle has reared its ugly head - money.   We need
money for stamps, paper and envelopes.   At the moment you are a
member of AIMS merely by associating yourself with us.   If anyone
has any ideas about raising money or can think of a rich patron I
shall be very glad to hear about it.   Please send me postage stamps
when you write.

Some people have suggested that we should wear a badge - do you
agree that this would be a good idea?

I hope that we can organise ourselves into "areas" under an
"area organiser" (any volunteers?) who will form pressure groups to
lobby M.Ps. and "chase" their Regional Hospital Boards.   I want
to compile a blacklist of maternity units that are known to fall
short of the standards required by AIMS (this list would of course
be cross-checked for accuracy).

Many of your letters so far are very interesting.   I will
therefore send you quite soon a Questionnaire which I hope you will
fill in good-naturedly even if you have already given me the answers
to some of the questions on it.

You will be pleased to know AIMS has the blessing of
Professor Norman Morris (of Charing Cross Hospital) who is being very
helpful.

An experimental Maternity Unit is to be built at Corby
(Nr. Kettering, Northants) and should be finished in about two
years time.

If an informal meeting were to be held in London in June or
July for those able to get there - would you come?   (A kind member
has a large flat she will lend us).   Would morning, afternoon,
evening or weekend be the most suitable?

It is important to keep writing to the papers, BBC and other
people even if you do not expect your letter to be published.   If
you do not wish your name to be published (some mothers say their
local hospital might "take it out of them" if this happens and they
need to go there again), then use a pen-name ("Mother of three" etc.)
and give your full name and address underneath stating clearly that
it is not for publication.

Light your candles and help to dispel this dark out of date
treatment - candles are used on people's birthdays - light yours
now to ensure that they commemorate a happy event.

Can you get five new members?

Yours sincerely,

Shelagh (Laura Main) and her son Timothy (Max Macmillan) with Sister Winifred (Victoria Yeates), who replaced Sister Bernadette in the Order.

SHELAGH

Shelagh started out in *Call the Midwife* as 'the little nun', Sister Bernadette. Younger than the other sisters, she had almost nothing to distinguish her beyond her diminutive stature, her spectacles and her exquisite singing voice.

She came into clearer focus in Series Two, when her owlish glasses were replaced with up-to-date, upswept eyewear, and as her tender respect for the widowed Dr Turner became apparent. Reprimanding Trixie for gossiping about the missing button on the doctor's surgery coat, she was later seen stitching a new one in place. This quiet gesture marked the start of an arc of extraordinary events,

which were to change her life – and that of the man she loved – forever.

Sister Bernadette began life as Shelagh Mannion, in the small town of Inverurie, Aberdeenshire. The daughter of a greengrocer, she trained as a nurse and midwife before experiencing the call to the religious life, and entered the Order of St Raymond Nonnatus in London in July 1948, just as the National Health Service came into being. From the earliest days of her career, she excelled in midwifery, being extremely adept technically and always maintaining a cool head in a crisis.

It was after the extraordinarily complex birth of Meg Carter's twin baby girls that Dr Turner and Sister Bernadette – who had worked side by side for an entire night – first exchanged personal confidences, and shared a sneaky

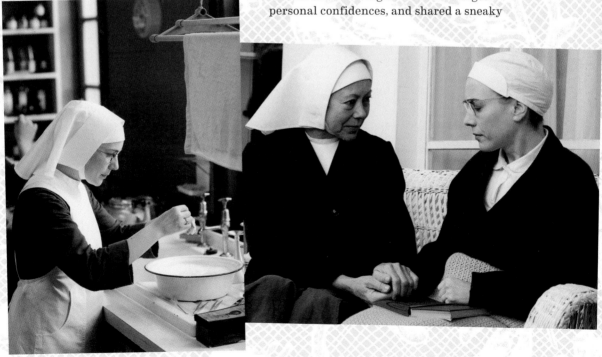

Shelagh and Patrick's love story had an additional, poignant dimension in their mutual fondness for Timothy, the vulnerable little boy who needed a mother as well as a father.

cigarette. Though Sister Bernadette tried to ignore her burgeoning feelings for him, she knew it was only a matter of time before they overwhelmed her.

In the event, it was Dr Turner who was overwhelmed first – in the parish hall kitchen, during the church fete, he kissed a graze on her hand. He was as shocked as she by his actions, and apologised immediately. However, they were unable to avoid each other completely, and time spent working together on the mass X-ray tuberculosis screening programme was to have unforeseen and devastating consequences.

Sister Bernadette was found to have several tubercular lesions on her lungs and was sent away to a sanatorium to recover. Dr Turner insisted on driving her there himself, but their parting was stilted, leaving everything unsaid. He wrote to her doggedly throughout her stay at the clinic, but she did not reply. Then, in one of the bursts of courage and commitment that have marked her progress as a character, a newly recovered Sister Bernadette telephoned Dr Turner and told him she was leaving both the sanatorium and her life as a nun. Theirs was a love that could no longer go unspoken.

When they were finally reunited, on a misty country road, the way ahead could not have been clearer to either of them. They began their official relationship with a simple exchange of the Christian names they had never previously been at liberty to use: 'Shelagh' and 'Patrick'.

Shelagh and Patrick's love story had an additional, poignant dimension in their mutual fondness for Timothy, the vulnerable little boy who needed a mother as well as a father, and whose handwritten plea – 'Please will you marry my dad?' – was central to Dr Turner's proposal of marriage.

As time passed, the couple's union grew in strength, despite – or perhaps because of – the challenges they faced. Shelagh, whose faith in God never wavered, initially struggled to adjust to life outside the convent. In addition, their first Christmas together was marked not by the quiet wedding they had planned, but an outbreak of polio that saw Timothy

fighting for his life in an iron lung.

After Timothy recovered, Shelagh intended to stay at home to look after her husband and delicate stepson, in the manner of most wives at that period in time. She longed for a baby of her own, but was heartbroken by the discovery that she was infertile. It became clear that her part-time role as medical secretary would not be enough to satisfy her in the long term – her passion for nursing, and for making a difference in the world, did not diminish even after she and Dr Turner succeeded in adopting their daughter, Angela.

Shelagh's medical training, skill and perspicacity have come to the fore time and time again since she returned to full-time work at the start of Series Four. She swiftly carved out a unique role for herself as clinic administrator, medical secretary and practice nurse. Her daily support for Dr Turner was never more necessary than when he suffered acute nervous exhaustion after dealing with a baby suffering from the bone disease

Osteogenesis Imperfecta. Running the surgery during her husband's illness, Shelagh donned the Nonnatus House blue and red nursing uniform for the first time – finally fully reclaiming her professional identity.

Across the *Call the Midwife* series, Shelagh's progress as a woman and as a character has been marked by changes of name, role and costume. Sister Bernadette's austere blue habit gave way to Shelagh Mannion's washed-out blouse and skirt, packed away when she took her religious vows. We have since seen her radiant in white lace as a bride, ironing in her slippers as a housewife, trim in her secretary's tailored suit, and swathed in a surgical gown as she helps new life into the world. She answers to 'Shelagh', 'Mrs Turner', 'Mum' and 'Nurse'.

But Shelagh Turner remains, above all things, herself – clever, sharp, funny, a tiny bit bossy, endlessly caring. An indispensable, loving partner to Dr Turner – and completely her own woman.

Dr. Patrick Turner

PHONE: POPLAR 491	GMC No. 89502	19 KENILWORTH ROW, E14

FOR .... DATE ....

CHAPTER 7

Outcasts:
the Currency of Shame

19, KENILWORTH ROW
E14
POPLAR   LONDON   ....

PRESCRIPTION No. ....

ABORTION

WHO DECIDES WHAT IS FORGIVABLE AND UNFORGIVABLE?

Especially when the answer is not a clean, surgical scalpel slice between right and wrong, but the kind of jagged tear that life can make into our best intentions.

This evening I've been rather silent; a lot to think about. I did something today that I deeply regret - to a person I feel deserves so much more. I can't believe my impulsive stupidity. Poor Timothy. He was trying to engage me in conversation about today's Summer Fete all evening, but I was hiding behind my work. Eventually he succeeded.

'Is it Mrs Harding and the herbalist? Is that why you're sad?' I looked up sharply. 'Who told you about Mrs Harding?'

Today I had to leave the Fete to attend to Nora Harding, a mother on my books. She was in a sorry state - an attempted, botched abortion. Her uterus had been perforated, likely by some back-street butcher. Blood loss was severe, and she had a worrying fever. I called an ambulance immediately. Her condition is delicate - both medically and legally.

'John Cotter heard his mum tell her friend,' replied Timothy.

The Cubs. Of course. Will parents ever learn that children have ears to match their curiosity? I put down my papers. 'Mrs Harding did something very sad, and which made her very poorly.'

'To her baby?' asked Tim. 'And to herself,' I said.

'Will she go to prison?'

'I don't know. But she might die.'

The last time I saw Nora Harding, she had asked for sterilisation. I couldn't help her, as our guidelines only permit such a procedure in cases deemed 'medically essential'. This was an exhausted pregnant mother of eight children – financially stretched, and clearly close to emotional breakdown. It's a bitter irony that the London is now treating the medically essential results of our previous indifference.

'John said she deserves to die because she killed her baby,' said Tim. He looked troubled. I put my books away and he sat beside me.

'Nobody deserves to die, Tim. But sometimes they do, and sometimes nobody is to blame. Sometimes doing the right thing can seem wrong, and doing the wrong thing can lead to something better.'

Later I tucked him up in bed and turned out his light. 'Do you forgive her?' he asked.

'Mrs Harding?'

'Mum. For dying and leaving us.'

I kissed his forehead on the pillow. 'I forgive myself for missing her so much. And loving her even more.'

I sat for a while in the kitchen afterwards. I thought of Mrs Harding's children, worried for their mother. I thought of Sister Bernadette, and how I might make amends. Condemning the chaotic outcome of the heart is as pointless as denying its existence.

We must apply ourselves to the relief of human misery, not simply to what we feel warrants our forgiveness. To do otherwise is truly unforgivable.

Condemning the chaotic outcome of the heart is as pointless as denying its existence.

On the face of it, the unfolding pattern of life was simple in the fifties. A chaste courtship was followed by an early marriage, with both parties sexually inexperienced. During adolescence women planned for a 'bottom drawer' of household items to take into married life, just as their mothers had done, and most expected to be grandparents in their forties.

Of course, these rigid social rules were often ruptured. But when anything outside the norm occurred it was women who were most likely to bear the weighty burden of society's moralistic disapproval.

Illegitimacy was the focus of immense shame and humiliation. Unmarried women who became pregnant were barely tolerated, even by their own families, while the men responsible usually remained anonymous. Whispered conversation about the arrival of illegitimate babies would include the words 'stigma', 'scandal' and 'sin'.

This was one of the worst manifestations of a male-centric society, but there were numerous others. Divorced men were seen as raffish, while divorced women were discredited, considered in the same category as unmarried mothers. Tax forms filled out by a husband permitted him to keep his earnings a secret, while his wife's were openly declared in his name. There were no joint accounts, and rarely did a married woman run her own bank account. She could not sign a hire purchase agreement or take out a mortgage on her own.

In this context, pregnancy – for some an against-all-the-odds triumph and yet for others joyfully routine – was not welcome news for unmarried women, and was a condition that needed to be reversed no matter what the cost. In the fifties in Poplar there were few opportunities to procure a legal – and safe – abortion, as outrage at pre-marital sex and a conception unlicensed by marriage was paramount in most people's minds. However, this sanctimonious attitude hadn't always existed.

Ancient Greeks and Romans accommodated abortion. According to Aristotle (384 BC–322 BC): 'When couples have children in excess let abortion be procured before sense and life have begun; what may or may not lawfully be done in these cases depends on the question of life and sensation.' In essence, he believed the unborn were in a vegetative state and then had an animal soul, before being endowed with a rational one.

There's little guidance in the Old or New Testaments on the issue, which probably explains why it barely featured on society's secular or ecclesiastical landscape until the nineteenth century. Indeed, a swift abortion – before the foetus moves of its own volition – appears to have been tolerated before that.

The tenor began to change in 1803 when the Ellenborough Act was introduced, condemning those who performed an abortion or obtained 'a miscarriage' to the hangman's noose, or 14 years' transportation. Abortion wasn't the sole subject of the Act; rather it was part of a raft of measures to stop malicious shootings, stabbings, poisoning and arson.

Illegitimacy was the focus of immense shame and humiliation. Unmarried women who became pregnant were barely tolerated, even by their own families, while the men responsible usually remained anonymous.

Bury

Incorporating the BURY & NORWICH POST

No. 9608 Est. 1782   FRI

'Dreadful danger people run when attempting abortions'

MURDER CHARGE REDUC
MANSLAUGHTER
'Extremely tragic, pathetic case'

AFTER hearing the evidence, Mildenhall Magistrates on Friday reduced a charge of murder against William Henry Goddard, a thirty years old general dealer, to manslaughter and committed him for trial.

Goddard pleaded not guilty to killing his wife, Flossie Ellen Goddard, on February 6th, and reserved his defence. At Friday's hearing, Mr. M. D. Hutchison, prosecuting, said the circumstances were extremely tragic and pathetic, for this unfortunate man caused the death of his wife by assisting her to commit an illegal operation on herself.

"And it may well be that the Bench will decide to commit him for trial on a charge of manslaughter, instead of that of murder, of which he now stands accused," he intimated.

Goddard lived with his wife and two children in a converted 'bus in Drove Lane, Beck Row, he said. The 'bus stood on a smallholding owned by a Mr. H. Hale. At 9.20 p.m. on Saturday, February 6th, Mr. Hale and his wife were sitting in their room when Goddard came bursting in saying "Get a doctor quick my wife is dying."

At the 'bus they found Mrs. Goddard sitting in a chair apparently dead. Mr. Hale's van failed to start, and he lent Goddard a bicycle.

Accused was in such a hurry that he cycled off in his stockinged feet to telephone for a doctor.

Goddard's first words to the doctor were "You are too late." Dr. Philip Harbin, of Mildenhall, found Mrs. Goddard was dead. Nearby were a rubber syringe, a bowl of warm soapy water, and blood-stains.

The doctor saw that it was a case of attempted abortion, and Goddard went to inform the police on his (the doctor's) instructions. Goddard said they thought his wife was about three months pregnant, and that she had done the syringing. The post mortem had revealed that the unborn child was about 21 weeks old.

Dreadful danger they ran

"Cause of death was air embolism (in the blood-stream)," continued Mr. Hutchison, "and this is one of the dreadful dangers people run when attempting abortions."

Air, forced under pressure, had entered the bloodstream and caused collapse and death.

Goddard had been perfectly frank in his interview with the police. In an alleged statement he had said: "I sat where I could see what she was doing, and when she was ready, I squeezed the syringe two or three times. She fell forward in the chair and her breathing became very heavy."

A very happy family

Goddard married his wife at Bawdsey in 1944, while he was in the R.A.F. They had two children, a boy (8) and a girl (5). They moved to Beck Row last August. They had been very happy since then.

Goddard had said in the statement: "We had no extra money, and no room for another child, so we thought this was the best way. I never thought it would end like this." On February 5th, Goddard had bought a syringe in Newmarket on his wife's request.

P.-c. F. G. Ruddock (Beck Row) answering Mr. Michael Havers defending said that Goddard was very frank about the whole affair. Without that he knew of no other evidence to show that accused had anything to do with it.

Had no idea of danger

Submitting to the Bench (chairman Mr. Donald Parker) that the charge should be reduced to one of manslaughter Mr. Havers commented: "Goddard had no idea of the danger; he played a very small part, and he could not have appreciated that serious injury or death might result."

An additional legal aid certificate was granted and Goddard, who is to go and live with his mother-in-law, was granted bail in the sum of £50.

Accused of killing his wife in 1954 after helping with a botched abortion, this father of two told the court: 'I never thought it would end like this.'

The sanctions originally applied only after 'the quickening', or when movement had been detected in the unborn child, but in 1837 the Act was amended so there was no distinction in the timing of the abortion.

Unfortunately, there was little available by way of birth control to stop women getting pregnant in the first place. And at the time an unmarried woman who was pregnant or had a child was likely to be hungry and homeless after being cast out by society.

There was a stark choice for women unable to legitimise themselves by marriage: they could either attempt to rid themselves of the foetus by home-spun methods or visit a back-street abortionist.

It wasn't therefore so much a medical problem, but a practical one. Everyday items to hand for those trying to get rid of an unborn child included gin, turpentine, raw spirit, aloe, sloes, crochet hooks, scissors and pickle forks. Newspaper advertisements promising remedies for 'menstrual blockages' were in reality home abortion kits, the worst of which used lead or mercury to induce a miscarriage.

These makeshift solutions meant that too often it wasn't only the foetus but the woman carrying it who perished, while survivors risked life-changing injuries such as blindness. In the decade after 1923, one estimate puts 15 per cent of maternal deaths as being due to illegal abortions. For this reason there were moves to end the suffering and deaths, and the Abortion Law Reform Association was established in 1936. It was one of several strands of a movement that appeared to gain momentum when, two years later, Dr Alex Bourne was acquitted of performing an illegal abortion on a fourteen-year-old

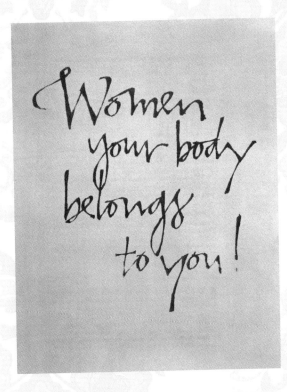

children to feed. There were rape victims, married women who'd had a fling, career women, schoolgirls and factory girls whose families relied on their income. Families keen to save face would disown a daughter who was pregnant and unmarried or, worse, commit her to an asylum. Women might have encountered men who sought incestuous relationships, and many who would not wear a condom.

During the sixties one young woman who was just about to take up a university place discovered she was pregnant. She contemplated using a knitting needle or a tampon soaked in bleach – and even thought of gassing herself like a fellow pupil at her school – before her desperate boyfriend stole the necessary drugs from a hospital and injected her himself. She said of the experience: 'It was horrible. All my muscles twitched and spasmed violently, I vomited uncontrollably – and then after a few hours I started to bleed. I was so relieved. It's hard to describe the feeling of relief that came over me.' Later, her boyfriend was fined for the theft. She said she had no regrets about

girl, the victim of a gang rape who was threatening suicide. He argued that the law did allow for abortion before twenty-eight weeks, and when a woman's mental or physical health was in peril. Yet the process still required approval from a psychiatrist before it could go ahead, until the Abortion Act – sponsored in Parliament by MP David Steel – became law in 1967.

This loophole had often been exploited by wealthier women prior to the Abortion Act, who had the wherewithal to consult the right doctor or could find the money for treatment at a private clinic. The Act came years too late for many of the less wealthy, though, who had died in agony at the hands of other women profiting from their woes.

Who was seeking an illegal abortion in the fifties? The number might have included women already struggling with a chronic shortage of cash and numerous

Families keen to save face would disown a daughter who was pregnant and unmarried or, worse, commit her to an asylum.

After Marie Stopes founded the UK's first birth control clinic in London her organisation went 'on the road' with mobile consulting rooms to reach as many married women as possible.

what happened, only that she had been forced to take such risks.

In 2004 a film by Mike Leigh called *Vera Drake* dealt sympathetically with a woman who performed illegal abortions in London during the 1950s. A loving mother and hard-working housekeeper, she took no financial reward for flushing out a foetus with soapy water, although the girls she visited had paid an unscrupulous 'fixer'. Jennifer Worth, author of the *Call the Midwife* books, was outraged and declared that this slant was skewed; she recalled her own memories of the botched abortions she encountered in Poplar. If there were tender-hearted women acting as a last resort in the best interests of desperate girls, she said she didn't encounter them.

Back-street abortionists were 'tough to the point of brutality' and were in it for the money. It was, after all, a risky business. Those who were caught 'fixing'

pregnancies, like Vera Drake herself, could be charged with manslaughter and receive a lengthy jail term.

'We, as midwives, were never directly involved but we often had to clear up the mess after a bungled abortion, especially on gynaecology wards,' she said in an article she wrote for the *Guardian*. Doctors, midwives and hospitals were duty-bound to report the victims of suspected illicit abortions to the police, although in practice this was never done.

'We all knew what the woman had suffered: prosecution would have been too cruel. But by shielding the woman, we were also shielding the abortionist, whom most of us would have wished to see behind bars. It was a dilemma.'

She recalled going into tenements to hear the stifled screams of a young woman ring out, shortly before unknown women scuttled away. 'A woman who avoided eye contact or hid her face if she saw one of the

Back-street abortionists were 'tough to the point of brutality' and were in it for the money. It was, after all, a risky business. Those who were caught 'fixing' pregnancies, like Vera Drake herself, could be charged with manslaughter and receive a lengthy jail term.

midwives approaching was in stark contrast to the cheerful housewives who greeted every midwife like a long-lost friend. We could never find out exactly what went on but we knew it was pretty grim.'

She took issue with the notion portrayed in *Vera Drake* that flushing out the uterus with soap and water was a quick and relatively painless way to carry out an abortion. 'The idea that a woman who has just had half a pint of soapy water put into her uterus could then get back up on her feet and walk around is utterly implausible.'

She said that abortionists knew quite well the hazards of 'flushing out', and that during her career she never saw anyone who'd survived that method. It was more likely that a more invasive procedure would be carried out, without the benefits of hygiene or anaesthetic, and using outdated or improvised equipment by unqualified people. The women and girls who were the subject of the abortion often had to be held down on the kitchen table as the pain was so excruciating. Once the foetus was removed it was wrapped in newspaper and burned on the fire.

However, Worth believed the fatalities after women had tried themselves to get rid of their babies were greater still. 'How a woman can push any instrument through a tightly closed cervix is more than I can imagine,' she said. 'But it has been done and I have heard so many stories in such diverse circumstance and they are all so dismally similar that the evidence cannot be doubted.'

Whatever the method of illegal abortion, there were long- and short-term risks to women that included rampant infection, anaemia, painful scar tissue, cystitis, renal problems, a torn cervix and even a perforated colon. Despite the horrors of back-street abortions, though, Worth was quite clear that the legislation that existed at the time was to blame – rather than the desperate women who sought abortions, or those that provided them. She did not regard it as a moral issue but a medical one; women who wanted abortions were prevented from getting proper attention.

The precise numbers involved are, of course, unknown. But given that birth control was often unavailable, it is clear the abortionists provided a much-used service. The lack of birth control and sex education – both of which might have severely dented the numbers of abortions – was another barrier being dismantled after the Second World War.

When the legislation that shaped the NHS was drawn up, it did not include provision for family planning clinics, the first of which had appeared in Britain in 1921. Marie Stopes opened her outlet in Holloway, London, after becoming famous by publishing a book about sex called *Married Love*, published in 1918 and written after an unconsummated marriage. The clinic's services were for married women.

A controversial figure who was a constant target of attack by the Catholic Church, Stopes nonetheless established a principle of 'children by choice' through

Marie Stopes was the public face of Britain's first family planning venture, aiming to prevent unwanted pregnancies among married women.

Despite the horrors of back-street abortions, though, Worth was quite clear that the legislation that existed at the time was to blame — rather than the desperate women who sought abortions, or those that provided them.

her support for women's rights. Further clinics opened, finally combining into the National Birth Control Association in 1931, and by 1937 there was widespread acceptance of their place in post-natal clinics. By 1958 there were 292 clinics nationwide, operating with the backing of Church of England bishops.

By the time family planning clinics started dispensing oral contraception in 1961, developed in America during the previous decade, it seemed birth-control clinics were an accepted fact of life. But now the spectre of the young and unmarried getting advice on birth control began to paralyse society.

As a consequence, the British Medical Association's journal *Family Doctor*

By the mid-fifties there were delicately phrased advertisements appearing designed to assist in family planning, which never mentioned the word 'contraceptive'.

advice she needs ..
yet hesitates to ask

When repeated pregnancies threaten health of the patient and welfare of her family, the physician's counsel is a timely safeguard.

In support of the physician's responsibility, a competent and skilful service is increasingly demanded — and secured by the traditional close alliance between ORTHO and the professional pharmacist.

DELFEN Vaginal Cream
PRECEPTIN Vaginal Gel

ORTHO-GYNOL Vaginal Jelly
ORTHO-CREME Vaginal Cream

ORTHO Vaginal Diaphragm

aiding the physician's responsibility in planned parenthood

Ortho Pharmaceutical Limited
Saunderton · Buckinghamshire

would not advertise the Family Planning Association, for fear of encouraging teenagers and the emotionally immature towards sexual practices.

In 1959 magazines featuring articles on the issue of unwanted pregnancies were pulped, while the BMA was accused of censorship.

Despite agreement on the Marie Stopes' board to sponsor a young people's advisory session at their clinic in 1963, a proposal the following year at the FPA annual meeting to extend contraceptive advice to unmarried women was rejected. However, there was support for youth advisory centres and, the same year, Helen Brook founded the first Brook Advisory Centre, exclusively for young, unmarried women. It wasn't until 1967, though, that the National Health Service (Family Planning) Act gave the green light to local authorities to offer birth control advice regardless of marital status, sweeping away previous prejudices.

For women who didn't employ birth control and then couldn't face abortion, there was the prospect of mother and baby homes, from which their infants would usually be adopted. There were scores of homes like these in Britain, typically housed within imposing Victorian

The British Medical Association's journal _Family Doctor_ would not advertise the Family Planning Association, for fear of encouraging teenagers and the emotionally immature towards sexual practices.

For women who didn't employ birth control and then couldn't face abortion, there was the prospect of mother and baby homes, from which their infants would usually be adopted.

buildings. Young women were sent there by their families or by GPs, usually six weeks before giving birth. Most stayed for a few weeks afterwards to recuperate.

It's impossible to generalise about everyone's experience, but the recurring themes in contemporary accounts are stark dormitories, chores and prayers. Crucially, the expectant mums would hand over their maternity grant to the home, to finance their stay.

This was the era before fertility treatment and, as a consequence, childless couples were often united there with small babies given up, willingly or otherwise, by mothers who had no way to care for them. Babies were parted from their natural mothers after hours, weeks or even months. Until the seventies there was no accepted route by which adopted children could later find their natural mothers.

Conflicted by the joy of adoption, Dr Turner nonetheless found conditions at the mother and baby home he visited unacceptable. He is haunted by the notion that previously childless couples leave there gratified, with a babe in arms, at the expense of the desperate young women penned inside.

Destiny, in a pink blanket: Dr Turner and Shelagh go to meet their adopted newborn daughter, Angela.

MOTHER AND BABY HOMES

'ILLEGITIMATE': NOT SANCTIONED OR VALID. A mean, spiteful little word – pasted across official documents and on the tip of respectable tongues. A red-hot brand with which to mark the blameless for the consequences of a natural but unauthorised desire. A man's desire, too, of course – but moulded as an instrument of purely female punishment. Shared sins carried in the single womb.

I'd always seen mother and baby homes as a necessary evil. Like an emergency ward, they were concerned with the pragmatic responses to events, and not their deeper causes. At best they could provide an unmarried mother and child with a safe and anonymous path from social shame. A young girl in trouble might go to full term and through adoption in privacy – returning to her life with a secret to hide, but without a stigma to bear.

The child? They might know an adopted innocence and prosperity beyond their mother's pain.

Tonight I lay with my little Angela. As she slept, I thought of the child's mother. The despair that drove her to give her child up for adoption – and the desperate hope that might still haunt her. Is she safe? Is she warm? Does love surround her to replace the shame?

I'd always seen mother and baby homes as a necessary evil … Until I saw Astor Lodge.

I was called out to see one of the young mothers, Denise Henshall. The place was in an appalling state: filthy, no electric power and stinking of neglect. The matron, Sister Maltby, had

I'd always seen mother and baby homes as a necessary evil...Until I saw Astor Lodge

deserted her post, fearing the consequences of my visit. She was correct to run. I was furious.

The half-dozen young women were crammed into a grimy dormitory. Denise Henshall had a nasty case of chickenpox, requiring urgent isolation. Another girl wept continuously. It was Dickens without the pity. Nonnatus House is to provide interim care over the holiday season, but the deeper stains won't wash away so easily. Astor Lodge had been a house of correction, not one of consolation or care. The illegitimacy of blameless children was to be borne by these women as a permanent apology. This was not pragmatism - it was a bully's vindictiveness.

As I looked from face to face, I saw Angela's mother staring back at me. The desperate hope that might still haunt her.

Can love replace our shame? Tonight I kissed my little girl, in honour of the mother who bore her.

There is nothing legitimate about a system that dispenses judgement without humility. Nothing sanctioned or valid about condemning an act without admitting the complexity of its cause. It is the very definition of misbegotten.

My child is as pure as the courage of the mother that brought her to me. As valid as the love she deserves.

My child is as pure as the courage of the mother that brought her to me. As valid as the love she deserves.

f British mother and baby homes had a dubious reputation, this was completely eclipsed by the horrors told about those in Ireland, the most infamous of which were the Magdalene Laundries run by various religious orders. Not only pregnant women, but also those guilty of minor misdemeanours were incarcerated in the laundries, which were commercial operations. Once inside their walls, it proved almost impossible to escape, with some women being kept there for years. Accounts of cruelty being meted out by the nuns are disturbing, and so too is the accusation that babies born there died unnecessarily and didn't receive a proper burial. There are also tales of a 'baby trade' with America. The last laundry shut in 1991.

Times changed, though, and unmarried mothers became more socially acceptable. Yet they were still a target in the eighties, when they were dubbed 'benefits scroungers', and again in the twenty-first century when the phrases 'unmarried mothers' and 'broken Britain' were frequently found in the same sentence.

Almost inconceivably, society found yet more ways to heap shame upon young mums who suffered puerperal psychosis. It's an extreme form of post-natal depression; only those lucky enough to be diagnosed would be given appropriate care in the mental health system. Even if their virtue was intact, however, neighbours had a habit of judging harshly new mums who could not care for their babies. Therefore a deterioration in mental health, no matter what the cause, was still seen as something to be feared and concealed.

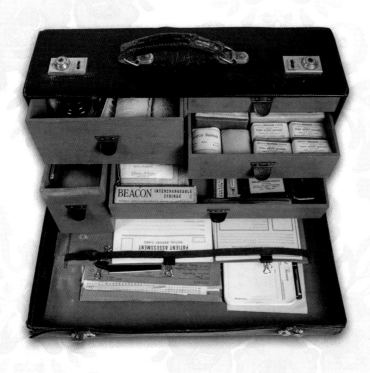

Magdalene Laundries and so-called training schools, like this one in Stanhope Street, Dublin, were run by religious orders and became notorious for the cruelty they showed to women.

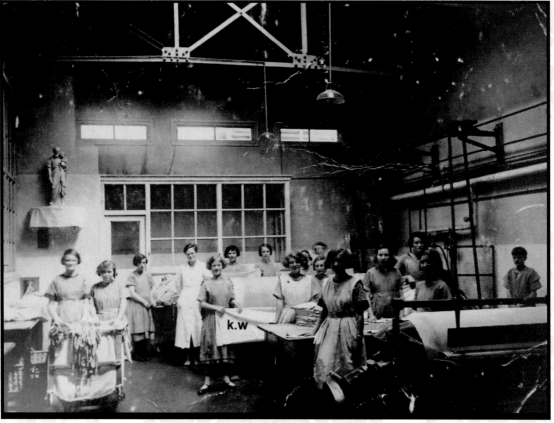

POST-PUERPERAL PSYCHOSIS

WINSTON CHURCHILL CALLED DEPRESSION THE 'BLACK DOG'.
Mr Churchill was right about many important things, but I feel he was
wrong about this. Profound depression is more like a black box than
a hound. A sealed case that imprisons the soul and isolates the self
from those we love. A place where no warm blood can penetrate - canine
or otherwise.

Pamela and George Saint greeted their new daughter, Rose, with
all the joy one would expect. A healthy child, born into love. What
was to come for Pamela Saint and her family was a rare ordeal few could
imagine, and no one should endure.

Puerperal psychosis is a severe mental illness that can strike
a mother after giving birth. Far more profound than post-natal
depression, it's a hormonal imbalance that devastates the mind. A
woman can develop mania, delusions, paranoia - moods and behaviour
that shock and confuse those closest to her. Worst of all, there's a
defenceless new life at its mercy. Finding and treating the condition
quickly is essential.

When I got to the Saints' home, it was clear that Pamela was
very unwell. I gave her a sedative and arranged a psychiatrist's
assessment. I saw that George was resistant to his wife's condition.
I recognised the ancient shame that cowers from all mental disorder
like a fearful plague. The key that seals the box shut.

The next time I saw them it was at a freezing dockside. If Sister
Julienne hadn't acted as quickly as she did, Pamela and her child
could have been lost to the Thames. Yet it seemed George was already

lost. He couldn't reconcile the fragile woman he saw as the wife he loved. She was admitted to Bow House for treatment - a place derided locally as the 'nut house'. It was a journey that - like too many others - she took alone: cut off from the love of her family by gossip, fear and ignorance.

Bow House holds hope, not fear. There is Largactil for her psychosis, and for depression she will receive electro-convulsive therapy. This mysterious procedure is as little understood as it is effective - a shock of light into the darkness, tearing open the box.

It's fitting that we endeavour to treat what scares us with something we don't fully understand. There's humility in it. An acknowledgement that the mind — like love — need not be wholly explicable to be fully cherished.

If George has the courage to open the box, he may find his wife more beautiful for her fragility - and find himself humbled by the journey she took for them all.

Sister Julienne (Jenny Agutter) pleads
with Pamela at the dockside.

Dr. Patrick Turner

| PHONE: POPLAR 491 | GMC No. 89502 | 19 KENILWORTH ROW, E14 |

FOR .... DATE ....

CHAPTER 8

The Legacy of War

19, KENILWORTH ROW
E14
POPLAR   LONDON   ....

D octors cared not only for the physical welfare of their patients, but also attended to their mental health. However, few GP surgery patients willingly admitted to an overpowering anxiety or a need for emotional help. Indeed, many didn't realise that the minor but persistent ailments that took them to the surgery in the first place were an expression of a far deeper psychological problem.

That said, there were a number of people – including war veterans – who displayed the unmistakeable symptoms of mental illness. As the fifties drew to a close, the sights and sounds of the Second World War still haunted the minds of many. When the six-year conflict ended there were more than 284,000 military personnel from the UK on the 'injured' list. But that figure probably doesn't include those who were afflicted by psychological problems, sometimes arising years later.

In addition there were large numbers of civilians scarred by what they'd lived through. In London alone 17,500 people were killed after it rained bombs during the Blitz. It was neighbours and friends of

As the fifties drew to a close, the sights and sounds of the Second World War still haunted the minds of many.

the dead who helped dig out the bodies. For the most profoundly affected there were mental institutions, which were typically spartan, joyless and dilapidated, with most dating from Victorian times. A number were prone to scandal over their shortcomings in care.

Inside the walls of mental hospitals there were treatments like electric-shock therapy – now known as electroconvulsive therapy (ECT) and still used today to help relieve depression, although much less often than in the past.

Some patients were lulled into deep comas by the use of barbiturates or even insulin. Happily, in the sixties, the number of lobotomies was already sharply decreasing. Just a decade previously numerous psychiatric patients endured

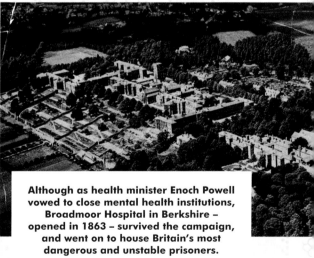

Although as health minister Enoch Powell vowed to close mental health institutions, Broadmoor Hospital in Berkshire – opened in 1863 – survived the campaign, and went on to house Britain's most dangerous and unstable prisoners.

ENOCH POWELL'S WATER TOWER SPEECH

When he was health minister, from 1960–1963, Enoch Powell set out his visions for changes in mental health in what became known as 'the water tower speech'.

'[Mental health units] ought for the most part to be in wards and wings of general hospitals. Few ought to be in great isolated institutions or clumps of institutions, though I neither forget nor underestimate the continuing requirements of security for a small minority of patients.

'Now look and see what are the implications of these bold words. They imply nothing less than the elimination of by far the greater part of this country's mental hospitals as they exist today. This is a colossal undertaking, not so much in the new physical provision which it involves as in the sheer inertia of mind and matter which it requires to be overcome.

'There they stand, isolated, majestic, imperious, brooded over by the gigantic water tower and chimney combined, rising unmistakeable and daunting out of the countryside – the asylums which our forefathers built with such immense solidity to express the notions of their day. Do not for a moment underestimate their powers of resistance to our assault.'

He declared that he would err on the side of ruthlessness.

'Hospital building is not like pyramid building; the erection of memorials to endure to a remote posterity. We have to get the idea into our heads that a hospital is a shell, a framework, however complex, to contain certain processes and when the processes change or are superseded then the shell must most probably be scrapped and the framework dismantled.'

These were tough words that mark a monumental change in the way mental health would be approached in Britain from that time onwards.

psychosurgery such as this, which entailed drilling holes in the side of the head and probing the brain with sharp spikes. Sometimes there was a subsequent improvement among those with personality disorders. Sometimes, though, the patient was reduced to a human shell.

Extreme measures like this became obsolete with the advent of new and effective psychiatric drugs, available both inside hospitals and out. The introduction of phenothiazine drugs in the fifties and the 1959 Mental Health Act at last began to reflect the depth of the issues being faced. The Act clarified for the first time on what grounds someone should be admitted to hospital against their will, entailing the use of an old-style straitjacket. The Act was also designed to break down the segregation that characterised the treatment for mental illness, thus lessening the risk of people becoming institutionalised.

But with mental health patients increasingly being cared for in the community, the workload and responsibility of family doctors expanded again. A shortage of psychiatrists – a relatively new branch of medicine – and psychiatric social workers made life harder for GPs. There was also a need for more training centres and hostels for the recently hospitalised people suffering mental health issues, as well as greater training for GPs in the field.

WAR NEUROSIS

A 'THERAPEUTIC COMMUNITY'. That's what the staff at Northfield military psychiatric hospital called it.

When I was admitted in April of 1944, the only thing I could commune with was oblivion. The person I'd been lay in a shell-shattered ruin somewhere south of Rome. What remained - that phantom stump of obliterated self - greeted the damp grey English hospital garden with a ghost's indifference.

War neurosis is a term almost genteel in its generality

War neurosis is a term almost genteel in its generality. It encapsulates every mental consequence of battle - every unique demon that can populate an afflicted warrior's personal hell. For some there's mania - for others, petrifaction. One might shake like a leaf in a bitter wind, another might fall into prolonged stupor. The grim thing that unites us all is the isolation of our condition - the solitary cell into which our frailties have thrown us, far from the fellowship of others. Horror makes a hermit of its victims.

Private Bryant's death had been the last act of my war: the last crimson flake that fuelled the avalanche. A ceaseless wave of butchered, broken flesh had poured into my makeshift surgery until it buried me alive. My life of healing had become an abattoir. There was no health left in the world. The Medical Corps discharged me and I was shipped off home for treatment.

Mental illness and shame have always shared a womb. Though I'd previously cajoled dozens of these poor souls with soothing words to dispel any sense of blame for their condition, my own self-hatred now rose like bile to replace the self I'd lost. The fellow patients who first welcomed me at Northfield were greeted with sullen silence. I'm glad beyond measure that they persisted.

Northfield was different. A patient wasn't an isolated recipient of psychiatric care but a member of a community that walked back to health as a group. The residents ran their own activities: newspapers, gardening clubs, bands. The psychiatrists used our little society as a way to understand us, and tailor their care to our needs.

I joined a small group of patients who helped out at a local child guidance clinic twice a week. The chaps would make toys, mend lights and offer extra pairs of hands to the nurses tending the mothers and children. I'd occasionally be invited to help wash the babies.

When you wash an infant, there's a serenity to it - a trust in eyes that have yet to know judgement or prejudice. Their innocence is a challenge to your despair - a timeless invitation to commune with life's possibilities, and not its fears. The more I washed those blameless little faces, the less blame I felt. Their companionship was the most merciful psychiatry. I left Northfield five months later - fragile still, but resolute in the fellowship of other souls. I was myself again.

Mankind is a therapeutic community. We heal ourselves together, or else we despair alone.

Mankind is a therapeutic community. We heal ourselves together, or else we despair alone.

Pulling together: Trixie and Jenny support a traumatised veteran and his wife after a bomb scare.

orthfield Military Hospital, where Dr Turner was a patient, was just such place. It was built in south Birmingham in 1905 as an annex to the Rubery Lunatic Asylum, and even had a green-domed water tower – which still exists today. More than 30,000 soldiers were treated within its red-brick walls during the two world wars. Two significant psychological experiments were conducted there, which helped define the future of therapeutic communities. The aim was to inspire communication with patients like Dr Turner by appealing to a sense of responsibility in the society in which they found themselves. Both experiments were notable for the imposition of military hierarchy, a factor eliminated from later therapeutic communities.

Soldiers returned from war not only with mental but physical reminders of the ordeal they had been through.

That was especially true for those men who returned from prisoner-of-war camps in the Far East. When Japan joined the war after attacking American ships at Pearl Harbor in 1941 its troops swept through the Pacific, taking thousands of British soldiers as prisoners. Afterwards they were held in primitive camps with insufficient food and poor medical supplies, while having to labour

> ## Soldiers returned not only with mental but physical reminders of the ordeal they had been through.

in inhospitable terrains. One in three is thought to have died. Those that returned were not only skeletal but were carrying a broad array of tropical diseases, some barely known in the UK at the time.

Experience garnered in the First World War had already informed Britain's medical establishment about the ongoing effects of malaria and dysentery. At the end of the Second World War doctors were again confronted with abundant examples of those conditions, as well as infectious hepatitis, dengue fever, hookworm, sandfly fever, typhus and cholera, and even smallpox. In addition there were still rarer conditions, including the *Strongyloides stercoralis*, the symptoms of which perplexed Dr Turner and inspired Patsy Mount. Like other tropical conditions, including malaria, it could lie dormant before erupting back into life, making diagnosis and treatment a challenge.

Aerial view of prisoner of war compound at Yokohama with a Curtiss Helldiver flying low overhead.

Nearly two months after the end of hostilities, 1,500 Japanese prisoners of war arrived in Southampton aboard P & O's liner _Corfu_ at Southampton. By then most were medically ready to return home.

STRONGYLOIDES STERCORALIS

WAR. WE CAN TRY TO FORGET IT, BUT IT RARELY FORGETS US.
Returning at our lowest times to haunt and harry. A worm that feasts on
those still living.

I've been dealing with a fascinating case: Maurice Glennon.
A veteran of the Japanese camps who'd been laid low by a back injury at
work. I'd prescribed steroid injections and left it to the Nonnatuns
to administer the care he needed. It all seemed very straightforward.
It turned out to be anything but.

Glennon is a crane operator at the docks. A good-humoured man,
with a caring wife and bright little daughter. It's not like him to be
idle, and he's been chomping at the bit to get back to work.

When Nurse Mount told me he'd become worse, I was surprised. But
she was right. A bad cough, fever and wheezing chest. I prescribed an
antibiotic to keep pneumonia at bay. Also I noticed a rather nasty rash
on his back, but didn't make any connection.

I was grateful that Nurse Mount did. She's new - wonderfully
forthright and diligent. When she suggested Mr Glennon's condition
might have some connection with his incarceration in Burma, I was
sceptical. Those appalling days are now sixteen years behind us
- long enough for even the most tenacious infection to show its
hand. Yet something in her quiet persistence made me put a call in
to the Hospital for Tropical Diseases at St Pancras. The response
astonished me.

Strongyloides stercoralis. A roundworm. Got into his body through bare feet while he was enduring that living hell in Burma. Worked its way up through the bloodstream to his lungs, then down into the intestines to hibernate for sixteen long years. That's where it would have stayed if I hadn't prescribed those steroids. They woke it like a careless spell wakes an old dragon in a children's story. Now it was back to finish him off.

Nurse Mount found it hard to accept Mr Glennon's dour prognosis - his likely death at the hands of an old invader. It seemed to energise her. Only later would I find out why. She took herself off to the School of Tropical Medicine in Liverpool and found a specialist who was trialling a new drug for treatment of Strongyloidiasis. Thanks to her, we now have a course of treatment for Mr Glennon, and a little more reason for optimism.

Extracting the past from Nurse Mount may be a little more complicated. I discovered today she'd been a childhood intern of the Japanese in Singapore and had watched her own family die in the camp. It explains her insights with regard to Mr Glennon; the restless energy that the feasting worm demands of the afflicted.

I know that restlessness. My hand is shaking as I write. The tiny tremor of a dragon's footsteps. Blood on Italian clay. Cordite and filth, and the spilt innards of the helpless. Never forgetting. Returning at our lowest times to haunt and harry. Still living.

Patsy (Emerald Fennell)
visits Maurice in hospital.

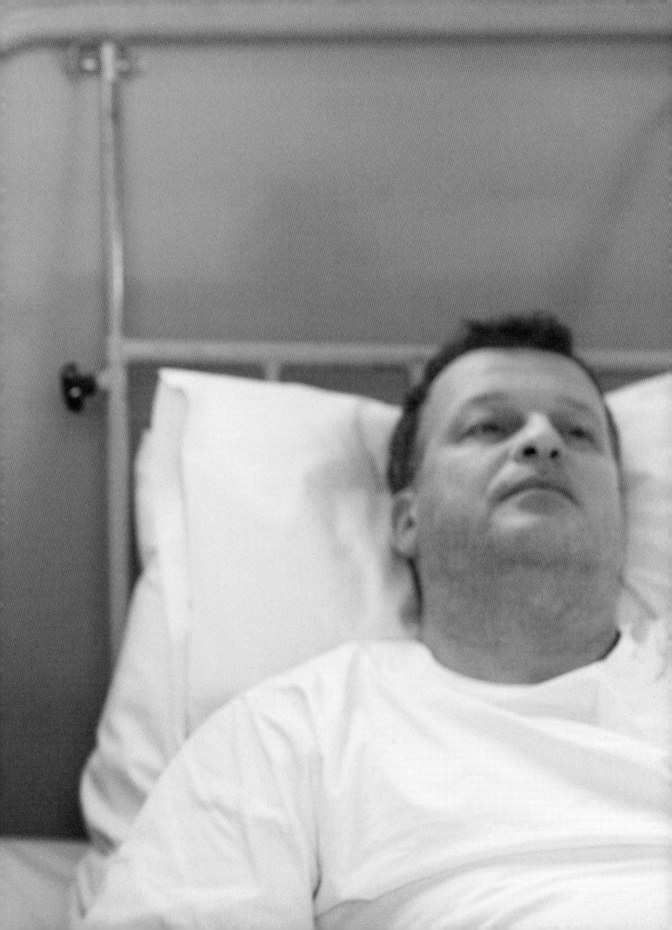

Dr. Patrick Turner

PHONE: POPLAR 491	GMC No. 89502	19 KENILWORTH ROW, E14

FOR .... DATE ....

CHAPTER 9

The Vaccination Story

19, KENILWORTH ROW
E14
POPLAR   LONDON ....

PRESCRIPTION No. ....

For centuries smallpox was a deadly scourge scything through populations, often in the company of armies on the march. A lethal illness, it killed at least a quarter of those infected, and left other victims horribly scarred. The first symptoms were fever, fatigue, aches and vomiting, with mouth sores preceding a virulent, painful rash that inched across the skin. According to a 1900 handbook of naval medicine: 'The pustules break, matter oozes out, crusts form, first on the face and then over other parts of the body.'

Acutely contagious, smallpox was nonetheless eradicated around the world by 1980 thanks to a sweeping vaccination programme that aimed to mop up every potential victim.

As early as 1959 the World Health Assembly vowed to wipe out the dreadful disease. Still, there was an outbreak in Wales in 1962, with six deaths, and a decade later a more substantial epidemic took hold in what was then Yugoslavia. The last known natural case was in Somalia in 1977. When it was diagnosed nearly 55,000 people were vaccinated there in just two weeks. Since then, the only known cases were caused by a laboratory accident in 1978 in Birmingham, England, which killed one person and caused a limited outbreak. To minimise the dangers from stored samples, only two vials containing the disease remain – in America and Russia.

The eradication of smallpox worked because sufficient numbers of people at risk from the disease were inoculated against it. So why haven't other diseases for which vaccinations exist also become old news? The medical problems in our world (and climate problems, too) can't just be handled as individual consumers but must be tackled as a whole society working together. We can choose to believe that there is 'no such thing as society' but a virus doesn't care about this. Victory in the delivery of post-war health provision was dependent on mass organisation to bring about maximum protection through vaccination – known as herd immunity.

We had to be methodical, plan carefully, be hygienic, set up health programmes with a view beyond the individual, in order to help everyone. The victory over smallpox was a high point in scientific planning and global thinking. There was no time to indulge that great first-world totem of 'personal choice'. Left to individuals – even rich ones – smallpox would still be a scourge now.

Should there be a laboratory accident now, involving those two remaining vials of smallpox, the risk would be huge as herd immunity against the disease (where a large percentage of a population is immune) is at an all-time low. It's vital to maintain herd immunity in diseases that are still present in communities today, as some people can't be vaccinated, including very young children and those with cancer. In this way wholesale vaccination protects those who can't protect themselves. Although the threshold among different diseases varies, the lowest bar is immunity in about 90 per cent of the population.

The vaccination story is one marked by triumph and disaster. Although

> **Victory in the delivery of post-war health provision was dependent on mass organisation to bring about maximum protection through vaccination – known as herd immunity.**

EDWARD JENNER: THE FATHER OF IMMUNOLOGY

Societies everywhere had been helpless in the face of a smallpox epidemic until British doctor Edward Jenner (1749-1823) derived a vaccine in 1796. It had long been held that milkmaids never contracted smallpox, suffering instead from the milder 'cowpox'. Jenner extracted the pus from a pox on a milkmaid's hand and infected an eight-year-old boy with it, through an incision in the youngster's arm. The boy thereafter proved to be immune from smallpox.

Despite the breakthrough, Jenner was widely mocked for what seemed to be a disgusting practice – inserting vile secretions into the bodies of children. But after more conclusive experiments, his notion won the day and Jenner coined the word 'vaccine', from the Latin *vacca*, meaning cow. The principle of vaccination – and its effectiveness – was established.

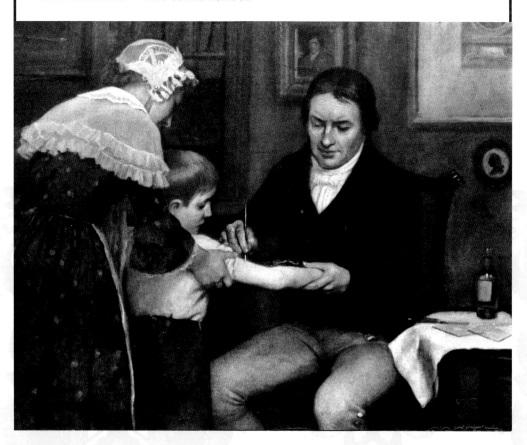

BAD OLD DAYS

The blue figures on the left represent our normal human population – healthy but unvaccinated. The figures in red are people who've become infected with something like measles or diphtheria. To the right we can see what quickly happens. Infection spreads by human contact – and because nobody has resistance, it simply spreads from one to the other until there's a whole epidemic of reds.

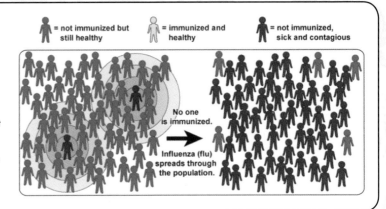

SOME VACCINATED

Now, in this one, we've started to vaccinate people – shown in yellow – but only some people. Those yellows will now be safe because they can't catch the infection themselves. But the infection doesn't care, because there are still enough blues for it to hop about from one person to the other, and get around the whole population. The result is still an epidemic.

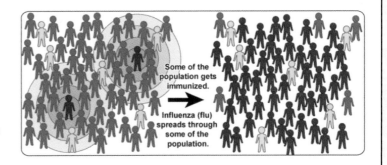

HERD IMMUNITY

But what happens when enough people get vaccinated? As you can see here, there are now too many yellows for those nasty reds to hop from one to the other and infect the blues. The yellows have become like a human shield of immunity that protects those last blues. The whole human herd is now immune. But why are there still any blues left? Surely we can just vaccinate everyone to be yellow? That is perhaps the most important part of herd immunity. You see, some people can't be vaccinated – even if they want to be. Young children. People with illnesses like cancer. Some of the most vulnerable members of our society. These people have to stay blue. So they need the rest of us

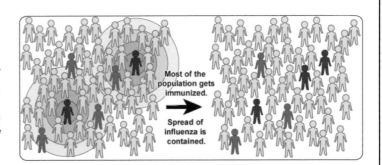

to be yellow in order to protect them. Herd immunity only works if enough people are vaccinated. The minute it falls below a certain amount of those yellows – bang! – the disease strikes again. Herd immunity thresholds are different for different infectious diseases but, generally, once it falls below about 90 per cent of the population, trouble starts. If you choose not to vaccinate yourself or your family, then you're not simply endangering your own health, but the health of the most helpless around you.

Jenner started the story at the end of the eighteenth century, it was the work of scientists in the nineteenth century that laid the true foundations. Most memorably it was Louis Pasteur (1822–1895) who established the germ theory of disease – stating that infection could be carried by microbes in the air – that significantly advanced medical knowledge. Also responsible for developing pasteurisation – enabling the safe sterilisation of food – his work on diseases undoubtedly saved countless millions of lives.

Pasteur was fond of reminding others that 'luck only favours those who are prepared'. His work prepared others, and it was mankind's extraordinary good fortune that so many strands of medical thinking came together in a short window of history.

Ignaz Semmelweis (1818–1865), who pioneered hand-washing; Robert Koch (1843–1910), who identified TB; Paul Ehrlich (1854–1915), who invented the arsenic-based drug Salvarsan that from 1910 helped treat syphilis; Joseph Lister (1827–1912), who introduced new standards of cleanliness and surgical practice and others put flesh on the bones of a new medical framework that gave hope to subsequent generations in the battle against fatal illness. Sometimes the work of scientists like these fell on especially fertile ground, as in the battle against diphtheria.

Louis Pasteur (1822–1895), who established the germ theory of disease – stating that infection could be carried by microbes in the air – significantly advanced medical knowledge.

In 1910, artist Richard Tennant Cooper (1885–1957) depicted diphtheria trying to steal a child in the night.

DIPHTHERIA

HOW QUAINT THAT OLD WORD SEEMS, YET HOW
SLEEPLESS AND DEADLY IT REMAINS. The names we think
we've assigned to the past can rise again to punish us.

ANZIO. THOMAS BRYANT.
I took up my medical practice after the war, armed with the greatest
weapon ever constructed to fight infectious disease. Vaccination?
Absolutely - but that was the bullet, not the means of delivery.

    The true agent of conquest was our collective will - an organised
desire to defend ourselves against infection as a single people. The
system of national health has enabled us to administer vaccine as a
population, not by individual proclivity: an essential condition for
mass immunity.

    Scourges like diphtheria attack the weak and the isolated
like lions after prey. To foil the hunter we must hide individual
vulnerability behind the herd's collective strength, and act
decisively to save those most endangered.

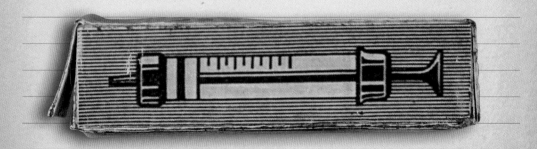

My past was laid to rest by the sight of their collective trust: my herd acting as one save our most endangered.

When I received the call from Sister Mary Cynthia, there was no time for hesitation. Ameera Khatun was nine months pregnant: temperature of a hundred and two, pulse racing, mucus stinking - her breathing constricted to a strangled rasp. Advanced diphtheria. Before vaccination was introduced in 1940, up to ten per cent of people who caught diphtheria would die from it. A grey-white membrane could develop in the swollen throat to block the patient's airway. Slow, agonising asphyxiation.

THOMAS BRYANT. EMERGENCY TRACHEOTOMY.

The field hospital in Campoleone was a roofless monastery filled with butchered screams and the stench of burned flesh. Bryant's jaw was shattered - he was breathing blood. An incision into the throat was the only chance his lungs had.

Nurse Gilbert and Sister Mary Cynthia hesitated when I told them that an immediate tracheotomy was needed to save Mrs Khatun's life. The ambulance had been called, but my hand had already reached for the scalpel.

I couldn't stop my hand shaking. The scalpel blade danced above Bryant's bloody throat. The captain screamed at me to do it. I willed the blade into his flesh, but the fingers trembled in response. The captain pushed me off, but Bryant had already bought it - breath expiring in a last gurgle of spit, blood and bile.

Ameera Khatun's throat lay beneath my blade. My fingers stiffened. The rasp of her breath punctuated the silence. I looked up. Nurse Gilbert was holding her patient steady. Sister Mary Cynthia was standing by with the tube, unwavering.

My past was laid to rest by the sight of their collective trust: my herd acting as one save our most endangered.

I sliced into Ameera's neck. I fixed the tube in place. Her breath broke free like dam water. She was safe.

The names we think we've assigned to the past may rise again to taunt us. Yet these old predators are no match for the wisdom of collective action. Infectious disease preys on our complacency. We must answer it with a tireless, singular will.

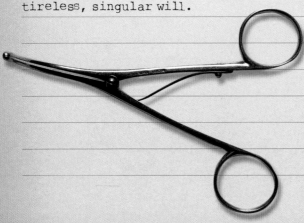

Scourges like diphtheria attack the weak and the isolated like lions after prey

Both doctor and father:
Dr Turner runs to
Timothy's bedside.

With children suffering a raging sore throat, it is possible to mistake diphtheria for scarlet fever. If their necks swell – well, that's a common symptom of mumps. But diphtheria has one tell-tale sign that will haunt both the afflicted and the medic who must deal with it. A thick, grey coating closes over the back of the throat which, if unchecked, can obstruct breathing, sometimes with catastrophic consequences. This is why an outbreak in Spain in 1613 is remembered as 'the year of strangulations'. Victims found themselves unable to draw breath, being throttled by vile mucus. The disease was spread by hoarse coughing and sneezing, and could also be present in bed linen and clothing. Children were most likely to succumb.

Pierre Bretonneau (1778–1862) coined the name diphtheria, taken from the Greek word for leather or hide (*diphthera*), which he felt described the tough membrane that the disease produced. It was Bretonneau who performed the first tracheotomy on a patient suffering from diphtheria in 1825. An early exponent of the germ theory of disease, he helped to distinguish diphtheria from scarlet fever.

In 1878 Princess Alice – Queen Victoria's third child and great-grandmother of Britain's Prince Philip – died from diphtheria aged 35 as the disease swept through Germany, where she was living. Five years later, Theodor Klebs (1834–1913) isolated the diphtheria bacillus. Within months Friedrich Loeffler (1852–1915) had published his work, having proved that there were more people carrying the disease than would be struck down by it. So clearly it was the poison it produced rather than the bacillus itself that was the problem.

Responding to these findings, Emil von Behring (1854–1917) started work on an anti-toxic serum that would at last help victims. The first Nobel Prize in Physiology or Medicine was awarded to him in 1901 'for his work on serum therapy, especially its application against diphtheria, by which he has opened a new road in the domain of medical science and thereby placed in the hands of the physician a victorious weapon against illness and deaths'.

Before presenting the award the Swedish chemist Count K.A.H. Morner said: 'I need not describe the terror which

> 'I need not describe the terror which [diphtheria] caused and the despair left in its trail in families from which it tore one member after another. Now, conditions are greatly changed and the picture can be painted in very much lighter colours.'
> **K. A. H. MORNER**

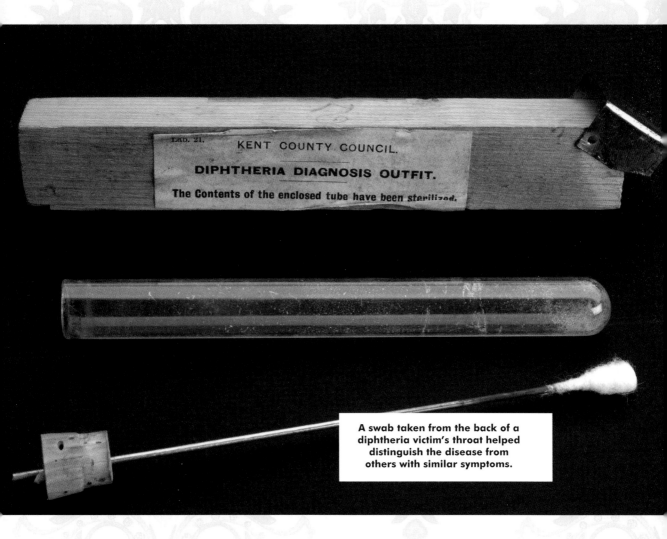

A swab taken from the back of a diphtheria victim's throat helped distinguish the disease from others with similar symptoms.

[diphtheria] caused and the despair left in its trail in families from which it tore one member after another. Now, conditions are greatly changed and the picture can be painted in very much lighter colours.'

With a vaccine and cure on the landscape, the outlook did seem much brighter, although croup, the barking cough that mirrored diphtheria, was still in evidence. In 1940 there were 61,000 cases of diphtheria in Britain, with 3,283 deaths. By 1957 the total had fallen to just 38 cases, with six deaths. But the disease has not been eradicated, as a major outbreak in Russia in the nineties proved.

Scientists and doctors weren't fighting on just one front when it came to chronic illnesses. Polio induced a particular terror when epidemics swept through neighbourhoods, especially among parents, for its association with childhood paralysis, withered legs encased in metal braces, the fearsome iron lung and death.

POLIO

NO. I WILL NOT LOSE TIMOTHY. NOT LIKE THIS.

The rhythmic wheeze of the 'iron lung' breaks the hush of the ward and marks the agony of uncertain time like a metronome. It's the only thing keeping my son in this world. I sit beside his unconscious face poking out of the gruesome contraption, as fragile and still as a corpse. I am helpless - my usefulness to him squandered by my own distractions. Shelagh - the wedding - my private happiness. I missed the signs. Now I must listen to a machine breathing for the child I promised to protect.

Poliomyelitis crept into my son's world undetected. The virus is a wicked one, striking the young and vulnerable and spreading like bush-fire in a tight-knit community like ours. Paralytic polio is rare, affecting only one in every two hundred. Yet it comes with rare cruelty. It switches off the body's motor - paralysing our muscles - even those we use to breathe. Suffocating from within. A ruthless thief.

The day we buried his mother, Tim was without tears. Like a breath held. He stood under my umbrella in soil-splashed shoes while his relatives looked on. There were compliments to his fortitude, and his polite responses earned sad smiles and old aunts' kisses. It was only in the night that the storm broke. He knocked on my bedroom door, eyes red.

'Can I sleep in your bed?' he asked.

I made space, and he lay where Marianne had lain until the pain stole the peace from her. The jagged rhythm of Tim's breathing marked time in the darkness.

'I'm scared a burglar might come and take Robert,' he said.

There had been a burglary at school the week before. Robert was Tim's goldfish. I leaned across and kissed his forehead. 'I'm here, Tim. I'll always be here. Nobody is going to come and steal Robert away.'

He held me tight. Eventually his breathing sank into the steady, reassuring metronome of sleep.

I've been campaigning about polio vaccinations for months. The national programme had been dragging its feet. I was due to treat the children in the New Year. Too late. The burglar had already left his calling card.

I keep vigil by the wheezing machine. If Tim can make it through these hours, paralysis can subside. Breathing can return - and walking, too, with help. Time and rhythm can be kind again.

When Robert finally died, Tim buried him in the garden with full honours - even playing a mournful tune on his violin as a send-off! I was scolded for not maintaining a suitably solemn expression. I later put Tim to bed and he asked me brightly: 'Can I have a new goldfish now?'

I smiled. 'Let's see what tomorrow brings.' I stayed with him as

he fell asleep.

Not Tim. Not like this.

Properly called poliomyelitis, polio is a virus that is spread mostly by poor hygiene – although contaminated water or food can also be its source – and for which there is no cure. Its initial symptoms are fever, fatigue, headache, sickness and stiffness in the neck, as well as a pain in the limbs, and its most likely targets are children under five. Often the virus would pass unnoticed, or else trouble the victim with uncomfortable but temporary muscle spasms.

However, when the illness evolved into paralysis, as it did for one child in every 200, it could halt breathing by stopping the chest's diaphragm from working. Those that were diagnosed in time were installed into 'iron lungs', or tank respirators, developed during the thirties to assist a

> Those that were diagnosed in time were installed into 'iron lungs', or tank respirators, developed during the thirties to assist a polio victim in breathing for a week or two or until they had sufficiently recovered.

polio victim in breathing for a week or two or until they had sufficiently recovered from its effects and could breathe for themselves again. The iron lung created a vacuum to reduce external pressure, making in-breaths easier to take.

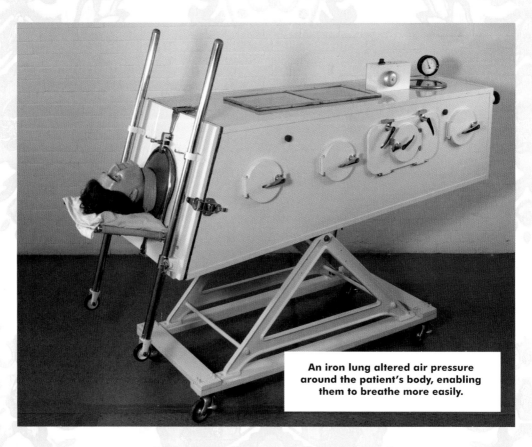

An iron lung altered air pressure around the patient's body, enabling them to breathe more easily.

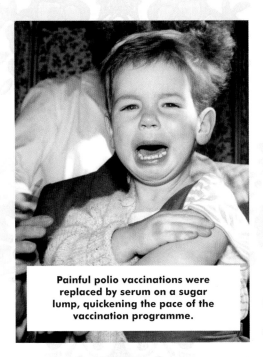

Painful polio vaccinations were replaced by serum on a sugar lump, quickening the pace of the vaccination programme.

Respirator, which looked like the chestpiece of a suit of armour and was much more portable.

Quarantines seemed to have little effect on the march of the illness during an outbreak, which usually occurred in the warm summer months. However, there were two milestone medical advances in the battle against polio in fairly quick succession, both in America. By 1954 a trial of the vaccine pioneered by Jonas Salk (1914–1995) was under way. The first trial had encouraging results. After the perfectionist Salk made changes, the vaccine was improved still further and offered 100 per cent protection.

Two years later rock star Elvis Presley received a jab containing Salk's vaccine, legitimising the treatment in the eyes of many young people.

In the sixties the injection was replaced by an orally administered vaccine developed by Albert Sabin (1906–1993); until this was universally adopted in Britain, polio was still claiming victims. In 1961 there were 707 acute cases and seventy-nine deaths. The government feared that the uptake of the polio vaccine was not as good as it might have been, and a new drive was planned.

In a 1962 *British Medical Journal* report, Minister of Health Derek Walker-Smith said that 'the level of immunity today in this country still leaves much to be desired and the time has come, indeed, is overdue, for the deficiencies to be made

Only the victim's head protruded. The person inside had to swallow with the rhythm of the machine, on an out-breath, to avoid choking. Coughing was more of a challenge because it was spasmodic, while the machine kept perfect time. Despite being the cause of hallucinations and the source of constant vibrations, people were often reluctant to leave the iron lung for fear they would not be able to breathe unaided.

Some polio victims never lost their reliance on the iron lung. When June Middleton died in 2009 aged eighty-three, she had spent more than sixty years encased in one, having contracted polio aged just twenty-two. June, who lived Melbourne, Australia, and suffered paralysis in all her limbs and her torso, was nonetheless pragmatic, once insisting: 'You've got to get over the obstacles.'

Other people held down day jobs but slept in an iron lung installed in their homes at night. For those who needed assistance from an iron lung on a long-term basis there was the Cuirass

> The concept of education or play on the wards was unknown. There were no bright murals on the walls or pictures stuck to windows. Indeed, a children's ward looked very much like any other ward. It was also a lonely place.

good. In a dozen areas 90 per cent of those eligible have been vaccinated but in others many young people under 18 years of age remained unimmunised.

'The first field trials of polio vaccine were carried out only eight years ago, which is a short time for the development of any immunulogical product. As new facts have come to light from technical developments and from vaccine trials, alterations have had to be made in immunisation schedules, which is often frustrating but nevertheless necessary.

'Salk vaccine correctly administered offers a good guarantee of protection to the individual but unless high levels of antibody are produced does not prevent the spread of virus in the community.'

There were polio outbreaks in Britain in 1947, 1950, 1952 and 1957. Most youngsters suffering from polio or similarly serious conditions stayed in the local hospital, a spell which for many caused as much misery as the illness itself; a child in hospital in the 1960s would have had a very different experience from one today.

The concept of education or play on the wards was unknown. There were no bright murals on the walls or pictures stuck to windows. Indeed, a children's ward looked very much like any other ward. It was also a lonely place.

In 1953 it was found that only 300 out of 1,300 hospitals allowed daily visiting by parents, while 150 actually banned it. Great Ormond Street Hospital in London, caring primarily for children, was one of the few that did not impose such restrictions.

The 1959 Platt Report said that parents should visit whenever they wanted – and should have a role in caring for their sick child. Still, doctors and nurses resisted the recommendations. It was vigorous campaigning by the National Association for the Welfare of Children in Hospital, formed in 1961, that finally helped to effect change. (In 1991 NAWCH was renamed Action for Sick Children.)

Even years after the Platt Report, however, children were still being taken into hospital with diseases for which there was an effective vaccine.

By the mid-fifties a vaccination that protected against polio was available. However, the hesitancy among Britain's population to have the necessary injection was a subject for concern in government and inspired numerous publicity campaigns.

POLIO

can cripple— even the fittest

**THE BEST DEFENCE
IS VACCINATION
IT'S AVAILABLE FREE
TO ALL UP TO AGE** ~~20~~ *40*

NOW

Ask your local health department,
clinic or family doctor for details

MEASLES

'IT'S ONLY MEASLES.' HOW I HATE THAT PHRASE.

As someone who has to deal regularly with the harsher consequences of the virus, I find it is never 'only' measles.

Little Tina Lewis was in an awful state today - delirious, burning up, not responding to visual stimulus. The scarlet rash had spread over her tiny body, and I couldn't even touch her without her flinching from my hand. By the time I put her in the ambulance I was fearing the worst - water on the brain. The Lewis family faces a Christmas full of pain and anxiety, while I'm helpless to relieve them.

Where the hell is that vaccine? It seems as though it's been on its way for years - yet here we are in 1961 and still nothing. Of course I understand that these things take time, but try explaining that to Tina's mother.

Measles is a heartless cuckoo of a virus. It starts with the familiar song of a less troublesome infection like the common cold - but by the time that rash appears in anger it's already spread to other victims and begun to do real damage.

There's a quiet, agonising toll of death from measles every year. Encephalitis can leave a child brain-damaged. Antibiotics have helped to fight infections caused when it strikes the body, but they can't stop the virus itself. So we wait until we can immunise - while children like Tina continue to fall like winter snow.

I've managed to get the local schools and groups closed over the holidays, so that should help. Measles is highly infectious, and remains so for days. Places where young people gather are the perfect breeding ground. Unfortunately, this has also scuppered Shelagh's Christmas choir preparations. She understands my reasoning, but I know she's taken it hard. I've resolved to do a little extra dish-washing over the festive period, but I doubt it'll compensate. I wonder if the florist has closed for his Christmas break yet?

Perhaps it's Mrs Lewis who really deserves a bouquet. Yet what good would flowers be? Decoration for a coffin lid? I do hope not.

The only Christmas gift worthy of Tina Lewis and her family is sitting in a lab somewhere, waiting for final approval. Inoculation. It's the one thing that might reduce a deadly scourge to something we can finally dismiss as 'only measles'.

easles, a disease that has played an infamous part in history, was typically problematic. It affected millions in the last century to greater or lesser degrees, causing complications including deafness, pneumonia and even death.

It was blamed – with other illnesses – for wiping out large numbers in the native populations of the Americas when European explorers first arrived. Those who had lived in remote locations in the New World had not encountered the virus before, and had not had an opportunity to develop protective antibodies. Westerners had the edge here; although they didn't know it, once they had been infected and recovered they would not suffer from measles again.

There was a breakthrough in understanding the disease in 1846, when Danish physician Peter Ludvig Panum (1820–1885) went to the Faroe Islands to observe an outbreak of measles unfolding. Although it affected thousands and killed more than a hundred, he saw that older residents who had endured the disease previously appeared immune. A later

'Here in Britain, because so many parents refuse either out of obstinacy or ignorance or fear to allow their children to be immunised we still have a hundred thousand cases of measles every year.

'Out of those more than 10,000 will suffer side-effects of one kind or another. At least 10,000 will develop ear or chest infections. About 20 will die.'

ROALD DAHL

US study conducted between 1912 and 1916 found that there were twenty-six deaths for every thousand measles cases.

Virologist John Enders (1897–1985) and wartime pilot-turned-paediatrician Thomas Peebles (1921–2010) began working on a measles vaccine at the same time as the fight against polio got under way. An eleven-year-old called David Edmonston lent his name to the vaccine after he provided the pair with a throat swab from which the virus was isolated. By 1963 the vaccine was available in America, where it was soon mandatory.

The innovation came too late for children's author Roald Dahl, who lost a daughter to measles in 1962. Olivia was seven years old when she contracted the illness and seemed to be on the road to recovery when she took a dramatic turn for the worse.

The vaccination against measles was effective yet some parents still persisted with the notion that the disease wasn't unduly harmful.

When his eldest daughter Olivia died, Dahl said he was 'limp with despair'. He and wife Patricia Neal had two more children after Olivia's death.

Writing about it in 1986, Dahl recalled that he was making animals out of coloured pipe cleaners with her when suddenly she appeared confused. Within an hour she was unconscious, and just twelve hours later she was dead. Measles, a familiar skin rash with a high temperature, had morphed into measles encephalitis, a deadly variation.

At the time there was no reliable vaccine available to counter measles. Much later, when Dahl wrote about the loss of his eldest daughter, one had long been pioneered but wasn't always being used.

Pleading for parents to recognise that measles was a dangerous illness, he sent out a blunt message.

'Here in Britain, because so many parents refuse either out of obstinacy or ignorance or fear to allow their children to be immunised we still have a hundred thousand cases of measles every year.

'Out of those more than 10,000 will suffer side-effects of one kind or another. At least 10,000 will develop ear or chest infections. About 20 will die.'

His vigorous support of the immunisation programme was countered by the prevailing point of view that measles wasn't serious. In an episode of a 1959 American show hosted by Donna Reed, one character announces: 'Measles ain't got no class. It's kids' stuff.' His biggest fear about having the disease was being laughed at.

Two years later, in an episode of *The Flintstones*, Fred Flintstone declared: 'Measles don't hurt'. And as late as 1969 in *The Brady Bunch*, the message from one of the children who had contracted the contagious disease was: 'If you have to get sick, you sure can't beat the measles.'

Many parents – having experienced measles themselves without any serious side-effects – saw little point in having their children immunised. Later this lethargy was fashioned into active opposition by a report published in the *Lancet* that linked the prevalent combined measles, mumps and rubella jab, used in Britain from 1988, to autism. Report author Andrew Wakefield was eventually disgraced after his theory was conclusively debunked. One only had to look to America, where every child had the combined vaccination, to realise that there were no detrimental health consequences of that nature. But Wakefield's disproved theory had the effect of deterring many from having their youngsters immunised.

So while polio has been eradicated from almost every country in the world (with the exception of Pakistan and Afghanistan) by a dedicated vaccination programme, measles continues to be rampant. According to the World Health Organization: 'The disease remains one of the leading causes of death among young children globally, despite the availability of a safe and effective vaccine. Approximately 145 700 people died from measles in 2013 – mostly children under the age of 5.'

Conversely, thanks to vaccinations carried out between 2000 and 2013, an estimated 15.6 million lives have been saved. The battle continues.

In order to protect everyone, we have to think beyond our own immediate self-interest. If we become a population incapable of basic altruism, then we will become a population once more plagued with deadly infections.

Vaccination is a moral tale for our times; a challenge to our innate sense of personal entitlement. It is a miracle that requires us to look beyond ourselves to be effective. Or it may be a curse that exposes our reckless selfishness and complacency – the squandering of the post-war legacy.

> Vaccination is a moral tale for our times; a challenge to our innate sense of personal entitlement. It is a miracle that requires us to look beyond ourselves to be effective. Or it may be a curse that exposes our reckless selfishness and complacency – the squandering of the post-war legacy.

Pillars of the community:
Dr Turner with curate Tom Hereward
(Jack Ashton), policeman Sgt Noakes
(Ben Caplan) and handyman
Fred Buckle (Cliff Parisi).

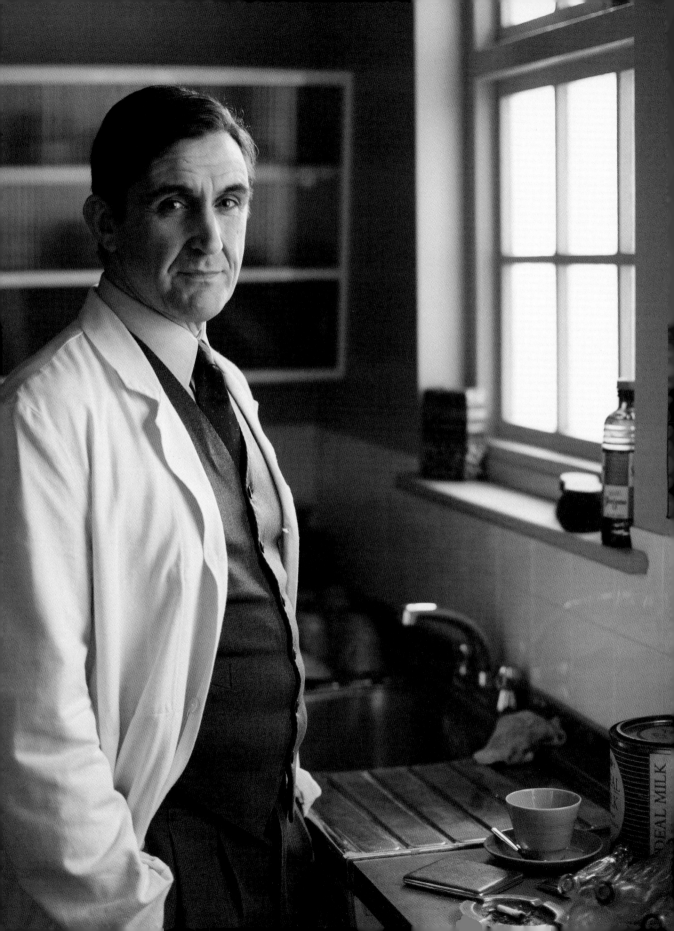

Dr. Patrick Turner

PHONE: POPLAR 491   GMC No. 89502   19 KENILWORTH ROW, E14

FOR ....   DATE ....

CHAPTER 10

Britain Cleans Up

19, KENILWORTH ROW
E14
POPLAR   LONDON   ....

KEROL
The *Guaranteed* DISINFECTANT

PROTECT THE HEALTH OF YOUR
Household by using KEROL—

the guaranteed disinfectant—in all cleansing operations. Soap and water cleanliness alone will not prevent infection, or keep your home free from illness.

When you purchase KEROL, you are buying a disinfectant of guaranteed strength and efficiency. Beware of the many worthless concoctions sold as disinfectants which have no disinfectant value whatever.

Your household is never safe from infection at any season of the year, therefore KEROL is a constant necessity.

KEROL is guaranteed to be 24 times more powerful than pure Carbolic Acid when tested against the Diphtheria bacillus.

A 1/- Bottle makes 30 gallons of efficient Disinfectant Fluid.

READ THIS GUARANTEE ON THE KEROL LABEL AND TRUST NO DISINFECTANT WITHOUT IT

KEROL
THE PERFECT NON-POISONOUS
Disinfectant

QUIBELL BROS. Ltd
NEWARK, ENGLAND

FREE SAMPLE COUPON.
See back page.

Nov 1910 WINDSOR MAG?

A growing concern with cleanliness helped improve Britain's health after the Second World War.

Medicine was enabling the performance of miracles by the fifties. With previously fatal diseases cured or prevented thanks to the appliance of tried-and-trusted scientific knowledge, there seemed little that could not be accomplished. For its part society was initially awed by these achievements, but then became a little complacent.

By the late fifties there was a whole range of new treatments, including pills for high blood pressure, steroids in the form of cortisone, Valium, and a host of other treatments to control troublesome conditions (some off-the-shelf remedies were more reliable than others). Little did people realise that some colossal health concerns still faced them.

GERMS MEET WASTE-PIPE WATERLOO!

For your home—
JEYPINE'S Pleasant Protection

For Outdoor Disinfection
JEYES' FLUID
Jeyes' Fluid—famous partner of Jeypine—is an 'outdoor worker'. And what a worker! For drains, dustbins, fowlhouses, etc., always use Jeyes'! Bottles at 1s. 0d. and 1s. 6d.

Wherever you suspect that germs *may* lurk call out Jeypine and—'Up Guards, and at 'em!' For Jeypine is indeed a safeguard for your home: it fights germs and *always wins*. But it is not harsh or pungent: on the contrary, it has a wonderfully pleasant pine fragrance that everybody likes. Get a bottle of Jeypine to-day: the price for a big bottle is 1s. — or_2s. for the Family size, with nearly 3 times the quantity.

JEYES' MAKE

JEYPINE
—*the better* PINE DISINFECTANT

With the germ theory firmly established, hospitals and housewives were keen to keep their environments as free from bacteria as possible.

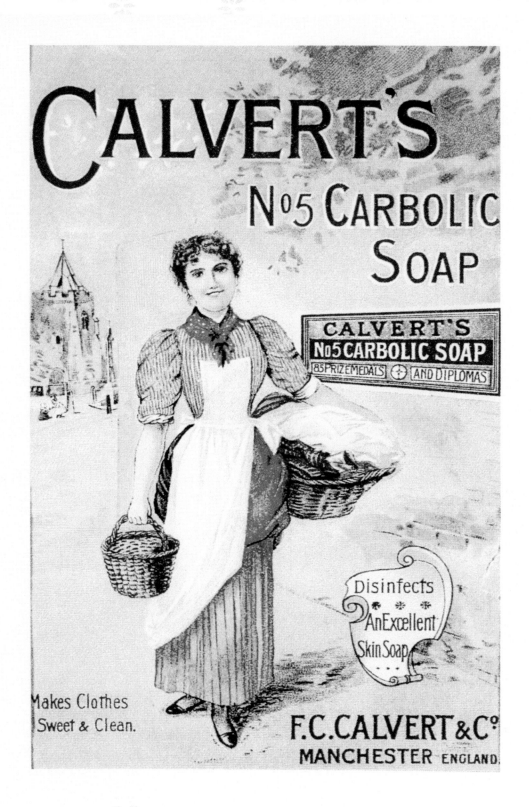

Joseph Lister had found carbolic acid to be a life saver in surgery conducted after 1865. Carbolic soap – containing phenols derived from petroleum or coal tar – was imbued with the same health-giving properties. It was commercially available in Britain from 1894.

DYSENTERY

THESE DAYS, IT'S OFTEN ASSUMED THAT THE EASIEST WAY TO HEALTH IS THROUGH THE DISPENSING OF MODERN MEDICINES. The doctor has become the arch magician - delivering his miracles in pill jars and syringes to banish all the evils of our parents' age.

If only this were true. In fact, the greatest threats to health remain those ancient maladies that haunt the shadows of a wider social blight: poverty, and the filth that follows in its wake.

I came face to face with one old ghost last week when I visited George Sitwell, a local locksmith. George was in a terrible state: delirious, and severely dehydrated from bloody diarrhoea. A classic case of dysentery - the ninth case in just two days.

Bacillary dysentery is an infection of the intestines, which is propagated by human waste - both faecal and social. It spreads rapidly where cleanliness is careless or is hard to maintain. It thrives in the overcrowded dwellings of the poor - showering its attention on those we've forgotten. Until soon enough we are forced to remember.

Shelagh has been invaluable. A dysentery outbreak requires not only carbolic soap and elbow grease, but also good detective work. The infection must be traced to its primary sources if an epidemic is to be contained. This takes a methodical mind and patience - something my wife possesses in abundance. She'd isolated one cluster of cases at Moffat Road School, but could find no connection with my locksmith.

Enter the redoubtable Nurse Crane. She brought Dolores McEvoy to my attention - an Irish immigrant living in dire poverty with her

Nurse Crane (Linda Bassett)

Nurse Crane could see beyond the magic tricks of medicine, and back to that ancient ghost that blights all the best efforts of our modern miracles. Poverty: the most resilient malady of all.

two children in Bulthorpe Hostel. Bulthorpe is a filthy women's lodging house by the river - a relic of a pitiless and resentful age. Dolores was in labour and found to be suffering from dysentery. The place was riddled with infection and infestation. Another cluster for Shelagh to ponder.

Bulthorpe was to be the clue that solved the riddle. The school and hostel had been provided with food from the same mobile catering business - G & A Domestic. Their chef was found to be ill with dysentery. The locksmith had visited the school and eaten with the children. The source of the medical outbreak had been traced.

Yet what of the social blight? Those dire conditions at Bulthorpe that maintain these diseases amidst the filth? Nurse Crane was adamant that the hostel must be closed. To my shame, I thought it a task too far. Yet close it she did. It's not every day I see our health officer Andrew Lansing shamed into action!

Nevertheless, his words still ring in my ears: 'Bulthorpe will exist as long as poverty does.' About this, at least, he was right. Nurse Crane could see beyond the magic tricks of medicine, and back to that ancient ghost that blights all the best efforts of our modern miracles. Poverty: the most resilient malady of all.

ysentery was one such problem. The disease manifests when bacteria invade the gut and cause diarrhoea as well as a fever, nausea and vomiting. As a result of the severe dehydration it causes, it can kill. Typically dysentery accompanied armies into battle and was certainly a major issue in the First World War on the Western Front, where sanitary conditions were poor. It could also be transmitted via shigella bacteria through cow's milk, before the era of pasteurisation.

Dysentery is also closely associated with typhoid, which had been even more notorious as a battlefield killer. Few people in Britain today know what it feels like to have typhoid. But many more have suffered from food poisoning from salmonella, close cousins of the virulent bacteria that cause typhoid, and they might have a good idea about its consequences.

Apart from stomach pains there's a headache and fever to contend with, as well as constipation and diarrhoea in turns. It might lead to inflammation of the heart, pneumonia, pancreatitis, a rash, kidney infection and psychiatric problems. Victims take a still greater turn for the worse if the disease burns holes in the intestines, which might lead to blood poisoning. Not everyone who contracts it will die, but before treatment was available the death rate was as high as three in ten people.

At the root of typhoid's spread is bad sanitation. It is passed between people via infected stools and sometimes urine. That means that fruit and vegetables grown using sewage-affected water might harbour the disease, as might food handled by carriers. Flies that have fed on infected stools can also spread it. It's therefore no surprise to learn that people living cheek by jowl with others are at risk. It is believed to have been responsible for virtually wiping out the population of Jamestown, an early settlement in Virginia, America, in the early seventeenth century.

Surgical Bandage

Width   B.P.C.   Length
inches   6 yards

Manufactured in England

In the East End, run-down housing was crowded into narrow streets, with a number of families sharing facilities such as toilets. The conditions meant diseases such as typhoid could flourish.

TYPHOID

IT'S A CRUEL BURDEN TO BE THE UNINTENDED VEHICLE FOR ANOTHER PERSON'S SUFFERING. Old Meg Mahoney is a fine, caring matriarch - the kind of mother who sustained life and limb in Poplar long before medicine was ever able to lend a hand. Having to tell Meg she was an undiagnosed carrier of typhoid was a bitter thing. Mrs Mahoney was deeply distressed to have transmitted a fatal disease to her neighbour - and although she couldn't possibly have known, the guilt of it clearly burns.

The typhoid bacterium prospers in human waste. Improved hygiene and sanitation have allowed our society to rid itself of an enemy that kills more effectively than bullets; yet in rare cases it remains a threat by hiding inside the bodies of unwitting carriers. These unfortunate souls may have successfully withstood a previous infection, yet they can still pass the fever on.

Thankfully, where there was once only fear and ignorance towards these unlucky people, we now have an official register of their identities. This is not to victimise, but to enlighten; carriers have very few restrictions, and simply have to observe common rules of personal hygiene. Nevertheless, discovering there is an enemy hiding within oneself is a nasty shock for any unsuspecting patient.

Meg is finding it hard to believe she can be anything but a fatal curse to her family and neighbours: a dreadful perversion of all the years of good she's done them. With our help she'll come to realise that her touch remains precious to those she cares for.

Discovering there is an enemy hiding within oneself is a nasty shock for any unsuspecting patient

We can all, at times, be the unwitting vehicles of suffering. Our accidents or errors can infect those around us with a pain we never intended. Yet this curse is more humanity than pathology - a reflection of the qualities of community, rather than an indication of any unique vice. Such hurt requires proximity: the unseen side-effects of a wilful care and belonging.

When we choose to live in common, we become a vehicle for so much more than isolated harm. We become the knowledgeable participants in an intentional good.

Diseases such as typhoid were rampant in the Crimea until hygiene pioneer Florence Nightingale (1820–1910) arrived at the Scutari barracks, and helped cut the number of deaths by instituting basic cleanliness. Still, 8,000 men were buried in the cemetery at Haydarpasa, in Istanbul, commemorated by an obelisk unveiled by Queen Victoria in 1857, a century before the time of *Call the Midwife*.

About 80,000 men who fought in the American Civil War also fell victim to typhoid; it was to the military that the first vaccinations were issued in 1896.

German professor Karl Eberth (1835–1926) had first identified the bacillus responsible in 1880. But that was only the start of a journey that would lead to a vaccine, containment and finally a cure.

Almroth Wright (1861–1947), who was in charge of the laboratory where penicillin was discovered by Alexander Fleming (and was later in charge of the laboratory with Fleming), developed a vaccine against typhoid that was tested on more than 3,000 soldiers in India and used successfully during the Boer War. As a result Britain went into the First World War with its troops immunised against it. For the first time, fewer British soldiers died from infection than from missiles. Still, in the absence of a major vaccination programme, typhoid continued to be a major health consideration as the nineteenth century closed and the twentieth century dawned.

'TYPHOID MARY'

One complication the disease presented was the existence of symptomless carriers, the most famous of whom was Mary Mallon (1869–1938). She was dubbed 'Typhoid Mary' after being the first person to be recognised as a carrier of the disease. Typically this happened when someone had suffered from it and then made a recovery. Only a few people were known to be carriers; small comfort to Mary, who was convinced the authorities had made a mistake.

Yet typhoid outbreaks had followed in her wake as she worked as a cook in New York. Irish-born Mary, who had emigrated as a teenager, was identified as the link in a chain of disease in 1907 and duly quarantined at Riverside Hospital on the city's North Brother Island. Three years later she was released on the understanding she never worked in kitchens again. Probably in the face of personal necessity, Mary changed her surname to Brown and got a job in a hospital kitchen. After a typhoid epidemic there claimed the lives of two people, she lost any public sympathy she had garnered when her role had first been exposed. This time she was exiled permanently to the island, and only left its shores after she died.

It wasn't just contagious diseases that were causing a problem in the fifties... Smoking was causing more health problems and premature deaths than ever before, as cancer exerted its grip on communities.

However, where there was a will, there was a way to get around the presence of the disease. A world fair being held in Chicago in 1893 was flagged up as a potential health hazard because the city's water supply was contaminated. Consequently, the city had almost double the average number of deaths in America from typhoid each year. After sending a delegation to investigate, Britain's *Lancet* journal advised visitors not to use ice in their drinks. This was enough to prompt the organisers to take action. Householders were urged to boil tap water, while tanks of sterilised water were provided. Ultimately fresh, clean spring water from 100 miles away was piped into Chicago to avert a crisis.

Even with the arrival of vaccinations, there were still difficulties surrounding transmission, and it wasn't until the advent of antibiotics that the disease was tackled decisively.

It wasn't just contagious diseases that were causing a problem in the fifties. Cancer, a complex condition with a long history, was revealing itself to be a new and terrifying challenge. At the time, cancer patients kept their diagnosis a secret, for the very word evoked fear and self-loathing. Even medics were naive in their beliefs, thinking there was a single

cause – probably a virus – and a single cure, at the time unknown. Medical treatments for cancer were highly toxic and not very effective. It wasn't until 1964 that American doctors began experimenting with drug combinations that some more significant successes were notched up.

Surgery was inevitably radical. It was years before earlier diagnosis through scans, focused surgery and new drugs prevented cancer being a death sentence. Smoking was causing more health problems and premature deaths than ever before, as cancer exerted its grip on communities.

Smoking was prevalent and, at the time, parents had no idea that they might be directly endangering the health of their children by lighting up a cigarette. Alarm bells had begun to ring at the end of the Second World War when lung cancer rates among women increased, shortly after the number of women smokers exponentially rose. But even then it was thought that emissions from cars, industrial smog and the tarring of roads might be responsible.

However, as lung cancer reached epidemic proportions, work in Britain and America pointed directly to a link with cigarettes. The perils of smoking were outlined from the early fifties thanks to the work of Sir Richard Doll (1912–2005)

STOP
don't smoke that
STICK

SMOKING
CAUSES DISEASE

CANCER, BRONCHITIS AND HEART DISEASE MAY FOLLOW HEAVY SMOKING

Although anti-smoking campaigns began in the fifties it would be decades before the message seeped into society's consciousness, thanks to the sheer number of smokers.

at the Medical Research Council, working first with Sir Austin Bradford Hill and later with Sir Richard Peto.

In 1950 one of his reports featured in the *British Medical Journal* was blunt. 'The risk of developing [lung cancer] increases in proportion to the amount smoked,' it concluded. 'It may be 50 times as great among those who smoke 25 or more cigarettes a day as among non-smokers.'

Despite this, and a number of other reports by Doll, the message was slow to seep into the public consciousness.

In 1954 Health Minister Iain Macleod met the press after one revelation and, smoking throughout, conceded that there was a dangerous link between tobacco and lung cancer. Despite the direct link proved by Doll and the others, government policy-makers were still hesitant to embrace the message, with Doll suspecting that high rates of smoking among journalists, television personalities and politicians was lessening their enthusiasm to spread the word. Sceptics thought smoking such an unremarkable activity that it could not be the root of such widespread misery.

The tobacco industry was listening, however, and in the fifties filter tips were introduced to ostensibly eliminate the threat. A survey led by Doll that focused on the smoking habits of 40,000 British doctors finally appeared to produce incontrovertible evidence, and in 1957 the

> To unpick the nation's smoking habit, that had often started in childhood and was perpetuated by a world war, would be a slow process.

'smoking kills' message was – finally – officially endorsed. Even then one doctor condemned the finding, declaring 'they will be blaming mother's milk next'.

To unpick the nation's smoking habit, that had often started in childhood and was perpetuated by a world war, would be a slow process. The sedate pace at which government moved on the issue – only banning cigarette advertising on television in 1965 and adding health warnings on cigarette packets in 1971 – didn't help.

There were numerous high-profile victims of the disease to fuel the messages fired off by the new anti-smoking lobby. Smoking was known to have played a part in the deaths of King George VI in 1952, Humphrey Bogart in 1957 and Gary Cooper in 1961. Writer Dashiell Hammett, a veteran of two world wars, was sixty-six years old when he died of lung cancer in 1961. In 1965 reporter Ed Murrow, often seen with a Camel cigarette in his mouth, died of it

In 1956 an edition of the *British Journal of Industrial Medicine* reported on the dangers of asbestosis and mesothelioma in London. In Poplar conditions were particularly perilous for dock-workers and their families.

too aged fifty-seven, as did singer Nat King Cole, at forty-five. The following year Walt Disney – a chain smoker – died aged sixty-five, and seventy-year-old comedy king Buster Keaton also fell victim to the disease.

A year before his death in 2005, Doll and others produced a report which said that men born between 1900 and 1930, who smoked only cigarettes and continued smoking throughout their lives, died on average about ten years younger than lifelong non-smokers. Those who gave up at sixty, fifty, forty or thirty improved their life expectancy by, respectively, about three, six, nine or ten years.

Medical experts like Sir Richard Doll and fellow campaigners conceded that it was hard to persuade people of the merit of giving up smoking. Even a later study that cemented the link between smoking and cot death did little to dissuade committed smokers.

Death rates from all cancers exceeded 100,000 for the first time in 1962, although the rise wasn't entirely down to smoking as there was a more noticeable prevalence in children. The main treatment was radiotherapy, although advances were being made in the efficacy of chemotherapy. Efforts were being made to combat the disease elsewhere, and in 1965 cervical screening began at five-year intervals for women aged over thirty-five. To complicate

matters, it was now known that smoking was not the sole cause of lung cancer.

In 1956 an edition of the *British Journal of Industrial Medicine* reported on the dangers of asbestosis and mesothelioma in London. In Poplar conditions were particularly perilous for dock-workers and their families. The report said that the wife of a docker had died of the disease after she brushed down her husband for years when he came home with his dungarees covered in asbestos dust. The authenticity of the case was questioned, with critics pointing out that no cargo was unloaded daily, and that working gangs were regularly rotated.

However, a 1964 report in the *British Journal of Industrial Medicine* stated: 'The latest data suggests that there is a considerable risk of men and women with asbestosis ultimately dying from a lung cancer.' It went on to say that there had been nine deaths from mesothelioma associated with asbestosis that year. Previously, deaths from the disease had been put down to lung cancer.

At the time asbestos was carried in hessian sacks. When asbestos dust escaped dock-workers complained that, on windy daya, it could be blown for a considerable distance, settling on the clothing of people away from the dock area.

Health and safety regulations gradually enhanced daily working lives over decades, and Britain finally cleaned up its act on child migration, which stopped in 1970. Following the war, 130,000 British children were shipped to Australia – not necessarily with the permission or knowledge of their parents – where they often ended up working as slave labourers.

There was perhaps a weary acceptance that age-old diseases might lurk in every dark corner of industrial London. But eventually the modern medicine which people trusted so much produced an all-new and shocking problem.

The hazards of asbestos were realised for the first time in 1928, as this cutting from the *Yorkshire Post* proves.

ASBESTOS DANGER.

Leeds Inquest Awaits Unusual Inquiry.

The possibility of an important medical discovery led to the adjournment of the inquest, opened in Leeds to-day, on Walter Leadbeater (34), of Aviary Mount, Armley, lately a labourer at the asbestos works of J. W. Roberts (Ltd.), Armley.

Dr. E. M. D. Greave asked for the adjournment, saying there was some doubt about the case.

"There have only been two post-mortems before in such cases as this," he said. "A doctor at Rochdale made a microscopic examination of the lungs in one case, and he thought there seemed to be a fungus of some sort there. I made a post-mortem in one case, and I believed it to be particles of asbestos. I hope to prove it is asbestos and not fungus."

Mrs. Leadbeater said her husband went to bed about eight o'clock on Thursday evening, and the following day she called in the doctor. At the works her husband could not wear a mask because he was short of breath."

The Coroner: An ordinary healthy man, not so affected, could have worn a mask, I suppose?—Yes.

The Factory Inspector: Was your husband gassed in the war?—No.

In the witness box, Dr. Greave said Leadbeater looked like a typical tubercular patient, he had a cough and was thin.

The Coroner: No one had suggested to him, apparently, that his work had anything to do with it?—He knew it bad, sir. He told me so.

Did you suggest something ought to be done about it?—I suggested he should leave and go into the open air, but the wages are extraordinarily good, and he was trained to it. His employers offered him a job where there was as little dust as could be.

In your opinion, the cause of death is bronchial pneumonia and fibrosis of the lungs due to asbestos dust?—Yes.

Dr. Greave explained that the examination was being made at the Leeds Medical School, and that the results would be known by Friday. This condition of lungs had never been known except in persons employed in asbestos works.

The Coroner: You are breaking new ground in this examination.

Mr. A. E. Whitham, a departmental manager at Messrs. Roberts' works, said that Leadbeater had suffered badly during the last two or three years, and had gradually got worse. Latterly he had been timekeeper.

The inquest was adjourned until Friday.

TEN PENNIES TO A SHILLING.

Leeds Business Men Disprove Proposal.

A proposal for the decimalisation of the shilling was mentioned at the Leeds Chamber of Commerce this afternoon, when it was stated that the matter might be made the subject of a resolution to the annual meeting of the association of British Chambers of Commerce.

Sir John Eaglesome said that however suitable it might be when applied to the florin, decimalisation of the shilling would not work. It would mean a penny of increased cost, but not of increased value. At best it was but a half measure, and what about the working woman who would only get ten pennies for her shilling?

It was decided that no action be taken on the suggestion.

OWNER'S TIP FOR TO-MORROW.

"I have not had a bet on the Grand National," said Councillor F. C. Parker, the well-known owner and backer, when asked for a tip for the big race, at a meeting last night of the Northampton Junior Imperial League, of which he is president

"However, you may do worse than have a bit on Terrible at Lincoln on Wednesday.

THALIDOMIDE

WHAT PECULIAR CREATURES WE ARE. We spend our lives lionising the rare beings who distinguish themselves from our own bland humanity. Yet when we meet some blameless soul bestowed by nature with looks that depart from acceptable conformity, we recoil in primal horror.

I'm ashamed to say I did the same when meeting little Susan Mullucks - if only for a moment. Our best guess is that baby Susan has a rare genetic deformity called phocomelia. The name translates, rather coldly, as 'seal-limbed'. The infant was born with malformed fingers and toes protruding directly from her torso - her arms and legs mutated to absence by some catastrophic error in foetal development. The cause of her condition is a mystery - but the effects on her family are all too clear to see.

Rhoda Mullucks is a strong and likeable mother of two healthy children. Her husband Bernie is a good father and husband. Their third child was expected to be a routine affair - the easy kind of joy that blesses our daily work. Yet life's most exceptional challenges can sometimes arrive in the guise of the familiar.

Shelagh was deeply disturbed by the child's condition - an unspoken affront to the harmony of the labour she'd attended. Susan had been hidden from her exhausted mother on a hasty pretext, and so I discovered the child lying alone in the side room - awaiting medical judgement in an isolation that spoke of our own shame, rather than the infant's welfare.

My only thought - as I gazed upon those tiny, twisted digits - was that she could not possibly survive. The physical malformation on the body must surely correspond to profound deformities of the internal organs. The registrar at the Children's Hospital advised that she was unlikely to survive the night, and so I was to monitor her vital signs until nature took its inevitable course.

Inevitable?

Who are we to translate what is written on the body as a judgement of the spirit?

Susan Mullucks did not oblige my malformed presumption. Her desire for life was as clear as the morning that followed. The child had chosen – and such a choice arrives with all limbs intact. All of its petals on display. The dandelion that mocks a lawn's dull conformity.

Once, at Nonnatus House, I had arrived to find Sister Monica Joan arranging a vase of wilting dandelions on the hall table. I made the mistake of referring to her bouquet as mere weeds. Her look would have withered far stronger plants than me.

'The weed is a martyred bloom,' she said, 'whose reputation is maligned by unfashionable appearance, unsuitable growth and an unappreciated vitality. The most effective poison to the weed is not man's science, but his ignorance.'

As I held the sleeping Susan in my arms, I was reminded of the sister's bouquet. There would be no martyrdom for this child. No fixation on extremities. Her growth was suitable – her vitality most appreciated.

Love finds a way: Baby Susan Mullucks, severely affected by thalidomide, is surrounded by her family.

At first the pill seemed pleasingly benign. A West-German pharmaceutical company, Chernie Grünenthal group, had produced a drug that countered the effects of convulsions by making users relaxed, even sleepy. So it was used as a sleeping pill too – and tests revealed that its toxicity was so mild that it was impossible to take an overdose.

Thalidomide also seemed to alleviate morning sickness among pregnant women – which could be so debilitating – providing a welcome remedy for GPs.

In mainland Europe it was sold over the counter from 1956, while in Britain it was licensed in 1958. In the UK, the most commonly prescribed drug containing thalidomide was called Distaval, manufactured by Distillers (Biochemicals) Ltd. Distillers took it from the German manufacturer, Grünenthal, as a tried-and-tested product, not requiring further research on their part. But no one knew the shortcomings in testing procedures at the time. Only when there was a spate of babies born with malformed limbs were concerns raised; it took until 1961 for the drug to be withdrawn. In that window of usage, an estimated 10,000 children worldwide were affected. Doctors had to confront a painful truth – that they had given patients a drug

> Doctors had to confront a painful truth – that they had given patients a drug that had catastrophically harmed rather than healed.

that had catastrophically harmed rather than healed.

The drug was present in a number of medications, including some cough mixtures, but the labelling did not use the word 'thalidomide', so it inevitably remained in some domestic drugs cabinets. At least 20 children were born during and after September 1962 showing typical thalidomide impairments – more than nine months after Distaval was withdrawn.

The manufacturer defended itself by pointing out that it had observed the testing standards of the era. However, the drug wasn't licensed in America after medical officer Frances Kelsey remained unconvinced by the available evidence about its possible long-term effects. Only 17 thalidomide babies were born in the US, after their mothers secured the drug from elsewhere.

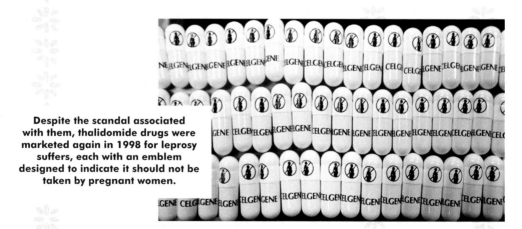

Despite the scandal associated with them, thalidomide drugs were marketed again in 1998 for leprosy suffers, each with an emblem designed to indicate it should not be taken by pregnant women.

In 1963 a two-year-old thalidomider walking on artificial limbs presented Princess Margaret with a bouquet when she visited the Chailey Heritage Hospital in Sussex. The hospital opened in 1903 as 'The Heritage Craft Schools and Hospitals for Crippled Children'.

On 24 September 1972 – a decade after the last victims of thalidomide were born – *The Sunday Times* finally published a story, labelling the treatment of thalidomide children as 'a cause for national shame' and noting that 'the law is not always the same as justice'.

Thalidomide campaign grows

THE Distillers Shareholders Group, which is fighting for more compensation from the Distillers Company for thalidomide children, said yesterday that its campaign is snowballing, writes David Blundy.

The Legal and General Assurance Society, which owns 3¼ million Distillers shares—about one per cent—pledged support for the shareholders' group last week. "We have had a lot of support from individual shareholders," says Mrs Sarah Board, chairman of the group, but the Legal and General represents a major block of them."

The General and Municipal Workers' Union, whose members work in many of the Distillers' plants, has also given its support. Mr David Basnett, the new general secretary of the GMWU, is to contract Sir Alexander McDonald, chairman of Distillers, to express his anxieties about the thalidomide children.

Ralph Nader, the American consumer lobbyist, has sent a letter to the chairman in Edinburgh, proposing that the company should pay $10 million (£4,225,000) a year for 20 years to the thalidomide victims. He suggests that the money should come from the company's profits or advertising budget and that Sir Alexander should make such an offer in a television broadcast.

Mr Nader says in his letter that if the case were being judged in the United States, each child would be awarded at least half a million dollars in compensation.

C.T.

OUR THALIDOMIDE CHILDREN: A CAUSE FOR NATIONAL SHAME

A Sunday Times Special Inquiry

TOMORROW WEEK, the civil law courts will reopen for the Michaelmas Term. It will be, near enough, the tenth anniversary of the first legal action taken to obtain compensation for children who were deformed by the drug thalidomide.

This may seem an apt—if none too expeditious—moment to settle the bulk of outstanding claims, and provide some disposable cash for 370 children whose afflictions date back to the early sixties. And it seems clear that in the new term, lawyers acting for Distillers Biochemicals, who made thalidomide, will appear with lawyers acting for the children, to seek court approval for a settlement which has been worked out in private over the past few months.

Unhappily, the settlement is one which is grotesquely out of proportion to the appalling injuries the thalidomide children suffered.

Essentially, the offer is that Distillers set up a trust for the children and their families, worth some £3.25 million.

This is not a large sum in the context of Distillers' commercial operations (a little less than 10 per cent of last year's after-tax profits, a little more than 1 per cent of the money made in the ten years since thalidomide). It may seem larger in the context of a claim for damages—until one reckons up the price of providing for a legless, armless infant who still has, in inflationary times, some fifty years of life to be endured.

No firm predictions can be made about individuals, for one feature of the trust is that no family can know what its own case will be worth. They have all been told that they must sign up "blind" or not at all. But there is a rough estimate that a family whose child is in the "top bracket" of deformity (that is, an entirely limbless trunk) might receive about about £15,000.

To put that sum in perspective, there is an actuarial estimate that such a case would need not less than £100,000 to support a reasonable existence over the likely span of life. And that estimate deals in the necessities of subsistence and special care: to provide the traditional compensation for "pain and suffering" would require a good deal more.

Fairly plainly, the proposed trust will be too small to make proper amends for suffering. Worse still, in the "top bracket" cases it will probably be insufficient to ward off simple destitution. Yet this proposed settlement is the result of much devoted legal craftsmanship, and its acceptance is being strongly—even passionately—urged, not only by Distillers' lawyers, but also by the lawyers acting for the afflicted families.

What has gone wrong?

In the decade since thalidomide was invented, marketed and withdrawn, it has become a symbol of the havoc that a technically complex society can wreak upon its own members. In almost every country where the miraculous new "tranquilliser" was sold, it caused a national disaster. In British terms, it was one of the worst of all peacetime accidents—worse than Aberfan, or the typhoid outbreaks, or any of our rare aircraft accidents.

Classic disasters tend to produce social reform, and thalidomide was no exception. A decade ago, it was possible for Distillers to promote thalidomide as being unusually suitable for pregnant women: Today, under the new rules which govern the pharmacological industry, such a campaign would be virtually impossible. Drug manufacturers must be much more circumspect in their claims.

Our new safety, of course, has been bought at the cost of several hundred distorted lives: essentially, the reason that the thalidomide victims are being

Mother pleads for drug babies
'PAY THEM COMPENSATION'

August 3, 1962

offered such slender recompense for their exemplary and involuntary sufferings is that, although their disaster effected a revolution in pharmacology, it has not yet caused any change in the system of law.

Yet the legal conventions under which this settlement was devised are already, by one good test, obsolete. The Law Commission, which is the body officially charged with proposing law reforms, has already decided that the present methods of fixing damages for personal injuries lacks "any mathematical, actuarial, statistical or other scientific basis"—and should undergo major reconstruction.

The Commission's proposals may never become law, and certainly will not do so in the coming Michaelmas Term. Equally certainly, Distillers are quite within their rights to fight their case hard, and defend their position, on the basis of present law, however absurd it may be.

Even so, our laws on personal injury and damages are notoriously ramshackle: almost certainly, they *are* going to be reformed. If, in the meantime, the most important of recent claims for personal injury should have been disposed of on an old and unfair basis, it would rank as one of the worst single failures of the English legal system.

IN THE ABSENCE of legal dispensation—which is the position for the majority of victims—the welfare state and private charity have provided much relief. But, significantly, Lady Hoare's Thalidomide Appeal now has difficulty in raising fresh money. The deformed births occurred so long ago that people assume the problem must somehow have been settled.

Yet the thalidomide cases originally generated a special sense of shock: possibly, because the deformities were often inflicted upon people whose intelligence and life-expectancy remained largely unaffected. The victims' sufferings are not, for the most part, to be mitigated by unawareness, nor curtailed by early death.

The sense of shock returns swiftly when details are re-examined. Here are the words of Mr Justice Hinchcliffe, describing the predicament of "David," a top-bracket case in which a settlement has been made:

"Each arm is represented by one very short bone. There are three digits on the right hand, the thumb and index finger being absent. On the left hand the thumb is absent and the index and middle fingers are fused together. There is no normal shoulder joint on either side . . . Each leg is represented by one bone. Both feet are grossly deformed and each foot bears six toes.

"In addition there is a congenital abnormality of the genitalia in that (1) the scrotum has not developed and (2) the one remaining testicle has not descended . . . But he is a bright and cheerful little boy of average intelligence . . .

"For all practical purposes he is immobile. He wears a very heavy 'flowerpot' prostheses with which he can rock himself a few yards. I saw him do this in my room. He certainly makes the best of a bad job. He can roll across the room at much greater speed, but then he cannot sit up at the end of his roll."

Not surprisingly, the judge believed that this boy, then aged eight, would face "appalling" emotional problems in adolescence, and would have no real hope of employment.

Judge Hinchcliffe is also worth quoting on the predicament of parents. Here he describes a mother whose son was born without arms:

"Mrs S——is obviously far from well. She is anxious, depressed and dependent on drugs to relieve her symptoms . . . she lives with a permanent cloud over her head. Sadness is the order of the day.

"She told the court that she felt 'up against the wall' . . . She has done, and is doing, the best that she can for the boy. It goes without saying that she will continue to do so in the future . . . It was Mrs S——'s intention to resume her employment; now this is out of the question."

THALIDOMIDE is a derivative of glutamic acid. It was developed in Germany, and made and sold here by Distillers under the names "Distaval," "Tensival" and "Asmaval"—just three of fifty-one names under which it appeared around the world.

The "story" on thalidomide was that here, at last, was a totally safe sedative and sleeping-pill: unlike the barbiturates, it supposedly had no toxic effects. This was, of course, a hideously mistaken proposition: in certain forms, thalidomide is highly poisonous, and in its ordinary pharmaceutical form it caused partial paralysis in many adults.

But while the story retained validity it appeared sensible to prescribe thalidomide to deal with the tensions—and consequent risks of miscarriage—which often occur in pregnancy. On a fair estimate, thalidomide probably caused deformities in about a half of the cases where a mother took the drug between the fourth and sixth week, the period when the foetus forms its limbs.

If innocence and pathos were decisive in matters of legal recompense, then clearly the victims of this error would have matchless qualifications. As things work out, it has been just the other way around. The claims of the thalidomide children have had to be pressed in the face of a great battery of legal difficulties.

Certain of their problems were, and remain, unprecedented in English law. In the nature of things, the children were unborn when their injuries were caused—and it can be argued that no one owes duties to a foetus which still lacks the legal personality conferred by birth.

Other problems arise from practice rather than principle: such as the judicial reluctance to admit the existence of inflation when computing the sum of damages. (Distillers is one of those companies which calculates the effect of inflation on its own profits. Yet Distillers' lawyers have argued vehemently that inflation must be *ignored* when fixing compensation for thalidomide children.)

But all these difficulties relate to something so basic that we take it for granted: that is, the adversary system of deciding injury claims. In English law, you get recompense for your injuries only if you can pin liability on some other person. If you are run over by a drunken driver who makes his escape, you may need money just as much as you would if your driver had stopped and given himself up. But you would not get a penny.

It is a difficulty faced in any personal injury claim—but it is raised to the *n*th degree by the size and complexity of the thalidomide disaster. Society offers the thalidomide families no remedy except to undertake lawsuits against Distillers: and if Distillers were bankrupt rather than prosperous, there would be no remedy at all. Equally, it is understandable that Distillers should contest those lawsuits vigorously, and strongly deny negligence.

In passing, it is worthwhile to note that the adversary method is not the only conceivable means of dealing with personal injuries. (Schemes can be devised, for instance, in which claims are met on a basis of need from a state-regulated insurance fund.) But the more immediate task is to set out a little more of the background to the present thalidomide dispute.

THE HISTORY of the litigation is immensely complex, but the salient point is that an out-of-court compromise was made in 1968 in the "test case" *S. and Others v Distillers Company (Biochemicals) Ltd.*

Richard, born without arms, sued, through his parents, alleging that Distillers were negligent in their testing and marketing of thalidomide. The allegation was withdrawn, upon an undertaking from Distillers to pay 40 per cent of the liability if the allegation had been sustained.

Essentially, this was because Mr Desmond Ackner, QC—now a judge, but then leading counsel for the families—thought that the chances of winning the case were significantly less than evens. When seeking court approval for the 40 per cent deal, he explained the two main problems that troubled him: "This action would have been the first . . . in which a child had claimed damages for injuries sustained before he or she was born."

There were criminal cases, he said, which were consistent with such a right of action—but no authorities. American courts had decided that unborn children had rights — but usually, with the proviso that they did not arise until the seventh month of pregnancy, when independent existence is feasible. (The thalidomide children were all injured between the fifth and eighth week.)

"What the Plaintiffs would have to establish," he said, "was that in English law a person such as a manufacturer of drugs, owed a duty of care to a foetus of whose existence he knows, or ought to know, from the very moment of conception."

To the lay mind, this might not seem a problem: all the same, Mr Ackner concluded that "success clearly could not be guaranteed . . . settlement must provide some discount for the possibility of failure."

Mr Ackner's other problem was: assuming there was a duty

SLEEPING PILL IS WITHDRAWN
'Abnormal Birth' Reports
BY A SUNDAY TIMES REPORTER

December 3, 1961

Thalidomide parents sue
A writ has been issued by the parents of a thalidomide baby, claiming damages against the

November 9, 1962

Delay on Thalidomide test case
DISTILLERS (BIOCHEMICALS) CO. LTD., a subsidiary of the

June 28, 1964

70 DRUG BABIES: BID TO SETTLE

November 18, 1967

£485,000 DAMAGES 28 THALIDOMIDE CHILDREN

July 31, 1970

of care, could Distillers be shown to be negligently in breach of that duty?

Proving negligence, Mr Ackner said, "would involve establishing that prudent drug manufacturers in 1958 tested this kind of drug, a sedative, on pregnant animals throughout pregnancy in order to ascertain the effect of those drugs on the conceptus, and that if such tests had been carried out the embryopathic character of the drug would have been revealed." It was patently a tall order; already, said Mr Ackner, the case had involved five years of work, and the examination of some 30,000 documents.

The 40 per cent deal in *S. v Distillers* has provided the outer framework of all subsequent negotiations. Conceivably, it was based on a pessimistic view—some lawyers would be more robust about the rights of the foetus, others less concerned about the contemporary practices of other drug firms.

Certainly Mr Ackner and his colleagues faced one of the classic problems of a legal system which operates by precedent. Their clients could only win by establishing a new precedent. No such case can ever be other than problematical: yet their clients, who had to take the risk, were people who could ill afford to lose.

"If the actions had continued," said Ackner, "the plaintiffs could have failed to recover a penny piece." Under the settlement, damages would in any case be "very substantial." It was, understandably, a case of taking the bird in the hand.

The next problem was that the bird turned out rather smaller than the plaintiffs' side had hoped for.

APPROVING the 40 per cent deal, Mr Justice Hinchcliffe said it reflected "great credit on all concerned." Originally, it was hoped that the two sides might be able to agree between themselves about how much the settlement should be 40 per cent of — but they could not.

So they went back before Mr Justice Hinchcliffe, and asked him to say what the total damages would have been in a successful claim for negligence. Two cases were considered: the armless Richard, and the armless-and-legless David. It was at this point that the plaintiffs case ran into serious difficulties, through a judicial refusal to take account of inflation, taxation and the actuarial technique of estimating life-span.

Mr Justice Hinchcliffe's uneviable task was to work out the amounts required to (a) compensate the boys for loss of earnings due to deformity, (b) provide for the costs of special care, and (c) give them some compensation for losing "the amenities of life."

The idea, in damages claims, is that the plaintiff gets a lump sum — which normally is invested. Then, by recourse to capital and interest, he is supposed to supply himself with appropriate annual payments. In the case of loss of earnings, the capital should run out at retirement age; in the case of special care, it should cover the probable life-span.

The judge heard much expert evidence about the educational and commercial prospects of the two boys, then aged seven and eight. He estimated that Richard, if born normal, would have been a prospective £3,000-a-year man, and David, if born normal, a £1,500-a-year man. He thought that Richard, lacking arms, would have only half his "normal" earning capacity, and David without arms or legs, would lose all of his. This, of course, meant that loss of earnings came to the same thing in each case: £1,500 per year.

After more expert evidence, the judge found David would need about £1,000 a year for special care. "This boy is never likely to achieve complete independence. He will need help for the rest of his life. He will never be able to toilet himself or to dress or undress. For all practical purposes he is immobile." He would need someone to wash him, dress him and drive him about: "Only time will show when and for how long during the day help will be needed."

For Richard, the cost of special care was covered by £250 a year. He would have to pay someone to help him off and on with his artificial arms.

The chief point the plaintiffs tried to establish was that the earnings they were losing, and the costs of their special care, would not be constant, but would be subject to inflation. This, again, was breaking new legal ground—at least, new at the time.

Professor Alan Day, of the London School of Economics, was called to say that a sensibly conservative estimate was that earnings could be expected to rise at not less than 6 per cent a year for the foreseeable future: this percentage being roughly half pure inflation, and half increase in productivity.

On this basis an actuary, Mr J. H. Prevett, FIA, calculated some tables showing lump sums required to provide for earnings and special care at various levels of award. He assumed that interest on the invested damages would probably be around 8½ per cent, representing a typical investment manager's "mix" of equity and fixed-interest securities.

Both sets of tables were discounted to allow for the probabilities of survival year by year: these discounts were made from mortality-figures for similar "lives."

In the case of David, Mr Prevett calculated that, after allowing for tax and inflation, the following lump sums would be needed:

Cost of special care	£51,792
Loss of wages.........	£54,974
Total	£106,766

In Richard's case, the figures were:

Special care	£12,925
Loss of wages	£47,504
Total	£60,429

The judge was quite unimpressed by this exercise—although it could be fairly said that its assumptions about inflation now look extremely conservative. Hinchcliffe said that he would stick to Lord Diplock's proposition that "money should be treated as retaining

CONTINUED ON NEXT PAGE

***The Sunday Times* conducted a long-running campaign to highlight how children affected by the thalidomide drug were being sidelined as the law prevaricated in the case.**

Nurse Barbara Gilbert
(Charlotte Ritchie)

Sister Frances Domenica, who opened the world's first children's hospice, was a nurse at Great Ormond Street Hospital at the time. 'Some of the mothers felt so guilty because they had taken medication. Some children had no limbs, others had varying degrees of deformity. In those days they were all shipped off to [St Mary's Hospital] Roehampton, to be fitted for prostheses, but these were difficult to wear. The makers tried to make replacement limbs look like real limbs, and they were very heavy.'

Despite the scandal, there was no official commission of inquiry launched by the government into how events had happened. There was a lengthy campaign to secure compensation for the children, who needed adaptations in homes and special equipment so they could live independent lives, but this encountered numerous hurdles. A legal case stalled, and while some guilt-ridden parents were reluctant to seek redress, others were deterred by red tape. Families buckled under the pressure.

When she was Lady Mayoress of London in 1960, Lady Hoare had established an appeal for those affected by thalidomide. She later became President of the Thalidomide Society. Several years later, with no appreciable progress made in the courts, Lady Hoare spoke out, calling it 'a tragic and deplorable' situation. 'Many parents feel ground down by prolonged litigation, degraded by the detailed form-filling they have had to undergo and deeper resentment of being made to feel they were going cap in hand for charity rather than moral justice from the wealthy Distillers.'

Attempts by British newspapers, most significantly *The Sunday Times*, to expose what was going on were dogged by legal action taken by the drugs companies.

On 24 September 1972 – a decade after the last victims of Thalidomide were born – *The Sunday Times* finally published a story, labelling the treatment of thalidomide children as 'a cause for national shame' and noting that 'the law is not always the same as justice'.

Today it's not the legal ramifications but the radical overhaul in the way drugs were tested that remains significant. Prior to thalidomide, every drug was welcomed as something beneficial and life-enhancing. Afterwards, drugs were greeted with far greater suspicion.

Perhaps curiously, given its unhappy history, thalidomide was later used for the treatment of leprosy, a particular cancer and some AIDS-related ailments. While its sale is permitted, there's always a risk that the drug will fall into the hands of pregnant women who will take it without appreciating the consequences.

The thalidomide episode was a body blow for GPs but it wasn't the only difficulty they faced. From 1961 London GP Dr Annis Gillie chaired a committee that looked into how doctors fared in post-NHS Britain. When the committee made its report two years later, it had some startling observations about doctors and their patients.

'His patients wish to place him on a pedestal as their chief – often their only – guide and counsellor ... Paradoxically their claims for help in day-to-day medical needs lead to his abrupt descent from this artificial height, especially where matters of prescription and certification are concerned ... An increasing number of patients are fully versed in some of the technological advances and many others have seen them demonstrated on television without a proper understanding either of the biological process or of the fact that in medicine there is very rarely black and white and all too frequently only minor variations of grey.'

The number of live births in 1962 was more than 25 per cent higher than in 1955 and the figure was expected to grow, according to the Gillie Report. By now families were beginning to disperse for work and family reasons, while at the same time the number of people living beyond the age of 65 was rapidly expanding. With families less able to care for the elderly, the burden fell to doctors and community nurses.

In 1963 the World Health Organization also looked into the future of general practice – and concluded that it was no surprise that students thought it dull or fit for failures. Medical school teachers should do more to challenge this view, it said. Nor was Britain the only place facing a crisis in its family doctor service. Thirty years previously in the United States there were ninety GPs to every 100,000 people. By 1963 the figure had dropped to thirty-seven.

The rumblings of dissatisfaction continued for the next few years in Britain, until a charter for the family doctor service was drawn up in 1965. It outlined the changes needed to re-invigorate GPs at a time when the majority were discontent with the extent of their workload and the way they were perceived in the wider medical profession. An injection of cash by the government was thought to be the best remedy, not least to provide premises and equipment. The government should act as banker and provide capital on terms that would give the family doctor an incentive to use it, said the charter, with repayment over the entirety of the doctor's working life.

Meanwhile the *British Medical Journal* trumpeted the needs of GPs at the time. 'If the trained doctor who enters general practice is to be able to do those things he has been trained to do then he must have adequate time, space and assistance with which to do them. In order to have these basic requirements he must find money to provide the space, equip it properly and engage the services of non-medical helpers who in their own special field of experience

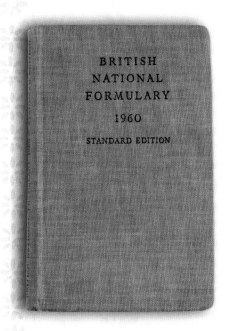

can take a good deal of work off his hands and so leave himself free to do that which he has been trained to do. Above all the general practitioner must have time to take a full history and make a careful examination of those patients who come to him with other than trivial ailments ...'

The *BMJ* went on to insist that GPs should have modern facilities at their disposal as they sought to diagnose the conditions presented in the surgery, time to update themselves on medical progress, and a twelve-hour day in a five-and-a-half-day working week.

To underline the strength of feeling among GPs, 14,255 letters of resignation had been received by the *British Medical Association*, which were to be activated if negotiations with the government about the charter failed.

Never a fan of the NHS, it was no surprise that the *British Medical Journal* ended the broadside like this: 'The Minister of Health should realise that doctors generally dislike working in the NHS in present conditions. The conditions should therefore be changed.'

'If the trained doctor who enters general practice is to be able to do those things he has been trained to do then he must have adequate time, space and assistance with which to do them. In order to have these basic requirements he must find money to provide the space, equip it properly and engage the services of non-medical helpers who in their own special field of experience can take a good deal of work off his hands and so leave himself free to do that which he has been trained to do. Above all the general practitioner must have time to take a full history and make a careful examination of those patients who come to him with other than trivial ailments ...'

KENNETH ROBINSON, HEALTH MINISTER 1964–68

Problems there might have been, but there were still those committed to the NHS, warts and all. On 15 September 1966 Health Minister Kenneth Robinson spoke rousingly at a meeting of junior doctors. 'What exactly is the National Health Service? It is quite simply one way – and our chosen way – of organising and financing the medical care of our population and in this the organisation and the financing go hand in hand.

'The objective is ... to try to ensure that medical care is distributed according to need; that treatment, the best that we can provide, goes first to those who need it most. This implies of course that health is not something that can be left to the economics of the marketplace or shared out in accordance with the ordinary laws of supply and demand. It is, I suggest, an ideal to be proud of and one which is very extensively carried out in practice in our own health service.'

He condemned those who trained in the UK then went overseas to work, where personal prospects seemed greater. 'Britain simply cannot afford to train doctors for the purpose of swelling the membership of the American Medical Association. This is emphatically not a burden the hard-pressed British taxpayers should be called upon to bear.'

But his defence of the NHS was stirring. 'Of course there are deficiencies, failures, shortages, and it is all too easy to pick them out and highlight them. They are inevitable in a vast service like ours, just as they are, say, in the education service. But slum schools are not news in the same way as slum hospitals are and we inherited plenty of those 18 years ago.

'No attempt is made to compare the service the British patient receives today with the service he got ten years ago or before the last war or with the service offered to the ordinary man in the street in the United States or France or Italy. Could it be that by any objective comparison of that kind our own service might come out rather well and the preconceived notions rather badly?'

He spoke of British doctors who travelled the world and came back imbued with renewed pride at the way the hospitals here functioned. His faith is still being rewarded, fifty years on.

TIMELINE

1796 Edward Jenner pioneers first vaccination, against smallpox

1847 Ignaz Semmelweis spots a link between maternal deaths and birth attendants with unwashed hands

1854 Louis Pasteur begins experiments with fermentation, leading to 'pasteurisation'

1865 Joseph Lister uses carbolic acid in surgery and on wounds, dramatically cutting death rates

1870 Concerned with animal disease, Pasteur develops a live vaccine for chicken cholera

1882 Robert Koch identifies the bacteria that causes tuberculosis

1895 X-ray machines help diagnose TB sufferers

1897 Aspirin is sold over the counter

1902 Midwives Act establishes training and protocols

1909 Albert Calmette and Camille Guérin develop the BCG vaccine against TB

1910 Salvarsan, the arsenic-based remedy for syphilis, is dispensed for the first time

1911 National Insurance Act provides sick pay and maternity benefit

1921 Britain's first family planning clinic opens

1928 Alexander Fleming finds the first evidence of penicillin in a petri dish

1928 Post-mortems reveal asbestosis for the first time

1936 Sulphonamides come on stream to treat infections

1936 Hospital trials proved that gas and air was the most popular pain-relief among pregnant women

1942 First vaccination against diphtheria becomes available

1944 Penicillin produced commercially by an American company for the first time

1948 National Health Service launched by Minister of Health Aneurin Bevan on 5 July

1949	Pethidine first used during childbirth for pain control
1956	Inactive polio vaccine administered by injection
1957	National Childbirth Trust holds its inaugural meeting
1959	Mental Health Act bridges the divide between old-style asylums and general hospitals, and introduces the concept of community care
1959	Platt Report encourages parents to visit children in hospital
1960	Association for Improvements in the Maternity Services is formed
1961	Birth control pill becomes available in the UK
1962	Live polio vaccine first given orally on a sugar lump
1964	Combination chemotherapy is used for the first time
1967	David Steel's Abortion Act is passed in Parliament, becoming law the following year
1968	Measles vaccine becomes available in the UK
1971	The first Computed Tomography (CT) scanner comes into operation, taking photos of the brain
1975	Ninety-five per cent of births occur in hospital
1975	The first whole-body CT scanner is built
1980	World Health Organization declares smallpox eradicated
1991	Back to Sleep campaign begins, to combat cot death

INDEX

Page numbers in *italics* refer to illustrations

A

abortion 37, 41, 148–54, *151*
Abortion Act (1967) 152, 245
Abortion Law Reform Association 151, *152*
actinomycin 113
Action for Sick Children 204
adoption 157, 160
Alexander, Albert 50
Alice, Princess 194
American Civil War (1861–65) 224
anaesthetic 30, 88
ante-natal care 83, 135
antibiotics 113, 206, 225
    penicillin 47–53, *52*, 224, 244
    sulphonamide drugs 53, 90, 244
Apothecaries Act (1815) 80
Aristotle 150
asbestosis 228, *229*, 244
Association for Improvements in the Maternity
    Services (AIMS) 136, *137*, 245
Astor Lodge 160–1

B

Back to Sleep campaign 245
Baldwin, Lucy 25
Barber-Surgeons Company 84
Barlow, Dr James 88
Barnardos 126
Barry, James Miranda 88
BBC 118
BCG vaccination *107*, 109–10, 115, 244
The Beatles 126
Behring, Emil von 194–5
beri-beri 74
Berlin Exposition (1896) 91
Bernadette, Sister see Turner, Shelagh
Bevan, Aneurin 80, 244
The Bible 150
Bing, Elisabeth 136
birth control 151, 152, *153*, 154–7, 245
Bissette, Abigail and Terence 98
Blease pulmoflater 25

bleeding, uterine 53
blood pressure 53
Bogart, Humphrey 227
bottle feeding 96
Bourne, Dr Alex 151–2
Bradford Hill, Sir Austen 227
The Brady Bunch 210
brain damage 119, 126
breastfeeding 96
breathing techniques 136
Bretonneau, Pierre 194
Briance, Prunella 135, *135*
British Journal of Experimental Pathology 50
British Journal of Industrial Medicine 228
British Medical Association 80, 155, 157, 239
British Medical Journal 112, 118, 227, 239
Broadmoor Hospital, Berkshire *170*
Brook, Helen 157
Brook Advisory Centre 157
Browne, Chummy 27, 40, 70–1
Bryant, Thomas 172, 189–90
Buckle, Fred *211*
Bull, Anthony 74
Bulthorpe Hostel 219

C

Caesar, Julius 88
Caesarean sections 30, 83, 88, 90
Calmette, Albert 109, 244
cancer 225–8, 238
carbolic acid *215*, 244
Carle Woodcock, Dr H. de 111
Carter, Mave 18–21, 139
Chailey Heritage Hospital, Sussex 235
Chain, Dr Ernst 50, 51
Chamberlen family 84, 86
charities 119, *119*, 126, 135
Charles I, King 84
Charles II, King 84
Charlotte, Princess 88
Chekhov, Anton 106
chemotherapy 228, 245

Chernie Grünenthal 234
chest clinics 112, *114*, 115
childbed fever 53
chloroform 25, 88
Chopin, Frédéric 106
Churchill, Sir Winston 91, 164
cleanliness 214–24, 244
co-operation cards 136
Cole, Nat King 228
Collins, Mrs 26, 28
Computed Tomography (CT) scanners 245
contraception 155, *156*, 157, 245
Cooper, Gary 227
Cooper, Richard Tennant *187*
cot death 32–7, 245
Crane, Nurse 216, *217*, 219
Crimean War (1853–56) 224
Croft, Sir Richard 88
Crooks, Will 68
Cuirass Respirator 203
cystic fibrosis 130–1

D

Dahl, Olivia 208–9, *209*
Dahl, Roald 208–10, *209*
Davis, David 88
death
    infant mortality rate 32–7, 83, 90
    maternal death 37, 42, 54, 83, 90, 151, 152, 154, 244
    stillbirth 90, 98–9, 123
    sudden infant death syndrome (SIDS) 32–7, 245
depression 162, 164–5, 170
Dick-Read, Grantly *134*, 135, 136
Dimbleby, Richard 119
diphtheria 187–91, *187*, 194–5, *195*, 244
disabilities 118–31, 230–8
disinfectant *215*
Disney, Walt 228
Distaval 234
Distillers (Biochemicals) Ltd 234, 238
divorced women 150
doctors, family 46–7, 64, 78, 81–2, 171, 239–40
Doll, Sir Richard 225, 227, 228
Domenica, Sister Frances 238
Domiciliary Midwifery Service 81
Donally, Mary 88
Down's syndrome 120
Dudley-Fisher 86
dysentery 216–21

E

East London Maternity Hospital 85
Eberth, Karl 224
Edmonston, David 208
Ehrlich, Paul 109, 187
elderly 58–63, 67
electroconvulsive therapy (ECT) 165, 170
Elizabeth II, Queen 65
Ellenborough Act (1803) 150–1
Enders, John 208
epidurals 30
episiotomies 83, 84
ergometrine 53
ether 30
Evangelina, Sister 48, 71, *71*
Eve, Dr 20

F

Family Doctor 155, 157
Family Planning Association 157
family planning clinics *153*, 154–7, *155*, 244
fathers 136
fertility treatment 157
Festival of Britain (1951) 65, *65*, *66*, 67
First World War (1914–1918) 35, 51, 176, 220, 224
Fleming, Alexander 49, 50, 51, 224, 244
Fletcher, Charles 118
The Flintstones 210
Florey, Dr Howard 50, 51
'flying squad' 81, 92–3
foetal monitoring 83
forceps 84–8, *89*, 90
Fordyce Turner, Dr C. 134–5
Franklin, Trixie 139, *174–5*
Funk, Casimir 74

G

gas and air *25*, 26–8, 30, *31*, 81, 244
general practitioners (GPs) 46–7, 64, 67, 171
    maternity units 81–2, 83
    and the NHS 80, 239–40
George IV, King 88
George VI, King 65, 227
germ theory of disease 187, 194, *214*
Gilbert, Nurse Barbara 98, 189, 190, 237
Gillie, Dr Annis 238
Gillie Report (1963) 238–9
Glennon, Maurice 178, 179, *181*
Great Ormond Street Hospital, London 204, 238

Guardian 153
Guérin, Camille 109, 244

H

haemmorhage 37
Hammett, Dashiel 227
hand washing 54, 115, 187, 244
Harding, Nora 148–9
Hare, Professor Ronald 50
Harper, Sally 120, 123, *124–5*
Heading, Robert 42
health standards 96
Heatley, Norman 51
Henrietta Maria, Queen 84
Henshall, Denise 160–1
herd immunity 184, 186
Hereward, Reverend Tom 98, 99, *211*
Hibbs, Lieutenant 49
Hill, Dr Leonard 111–12
Hoare, Lady 238
home births *31*, 90
    advantages of 134
    in the 1950s and 1960s 24–5, 31, 81, 82–4
home confinement grants 82–3
home visits 47
hospital, children in 178, 245
hospital births 82–4, 90, 245
    maternity units 81, 82
    opposition to 134–6
    pain relief 30–1
Hospital for Tropical Diseases London 178
Human Tissue Act (1961) 37
Hunt, Mary 51
The Hurt Mind 118
hygiene
    in childbirth 84, 90, 91
    and diseases 115, 202, 214–24
    handwashing 54, 187, 244
    at home 96

I

illegitimacy 150, 151, 160
immunisation *see* vaccinations
Imperial Chemical Industries (ICI) 25
incubators 91, *91*
induction 83–4
infant mortality rate 32–7, 83, 90
International Journal of Epidemiology 35
International Military Tribunal 37

intervention methods 83–4
    Caesarean sections 30, 83, 88, 90
    forceps 84–8, *89*, 90
    NCT lobbies against 135
iron lungs 195, 196, 202–3, *202*

J

Jenkins, Mrs Mary Anne *60–1*, 62
Jenner, Edward 185, 187, 244
Johnson, Eric 31
Jones, Margaret 40
Julienne, Sister 32, 164

K

Kafka, Franz 106
Keaton, Buster 228
Keats, John 106
Kelly, Patrick and Rene 32–4
Kelsey, Frances 234
Khatun, Ameera 189, 190
Klebs, Theodor 194
Koch, Robert 106–9, *107*, 111, 115, 187, 244

L

labour, quickening 53
Lamaze, Dr Ferdinand 136
Lamaze method 136
Lancet 210, 225
Lansbury, George 67, 68
Lansbury Estate, Poplar 65, *65, 66*, 67
Lansing, Andrew 219
Largactil 165
Lee, Nurse Jenny 128, *174–5*
Leopold, Prince 25
leprosy *234*, 238
Lewis, Tina 206–7
Lister, Joseph 187, *215*, 244
Live Architecture Exhibition (1951) 67
live birth rate 238–9
Loeffler, Friedrich 194
Longfellow, Fanny 30
Longfellow, Henry Wadsworth 30
lung cancer 225–8
'lying-in' 31, 82
lysozyme 50

M

McEntie, Brenda 70–1
McEvoy, Dolores 216

Macleod, Iain 227
Magdalene Laundries 162, *163*
Mahoney, Meg 222
Mallon, Mary 'Typhoid Mary' 224
malnutrition 54
Maltby, Sister 160
Mantoux test 109
Margaret, Princess *235*
Marie Curie Cancer Care 126
Marie Stopes *153*, 154–5, *155*, 157
Mary Cynthia, Sister 189, 190
massage 136
maternal death 37, 83, 244
  abortions 151, 152, 154
  and hygiene 54
  pre-eclampsia 42
  sulphonamide drugs 53
Maternity and Midwifery Advisory Committee 83
maternity grants 82, 83, 157, 244
Maternity Services Committee 30–1, 82
maternity units 81–2, 83
measles 206–10, 245
mental health 118, 162, 164–5, 170–6
Mental Health Act (1959) 171, 245
mesothelioma 228
Middleton, June 203
midwifery 78, 80
Midwives Act (1902) 78, 244
milk 96, 112–13
Miller, Nurse 32, 34, *38*, 40, 123
Milligan, Jacob 123
Ministry of Health *36*, 78
miscarriages 150–1
MMR 210
Monica Joan, Sister 48, 49, 130–1, *131*, 231
Morner, Count K.A.H. 194–5
morning sickness 234
mortality rates
  infant mortality rate 32–7, 83, 90
  maternal death 37, 42, 54, 83, 90, 151, 152, 154, 244
mother and baby homes 157, 160–3
Mount, Nurse Patsy 98, 176, 178, 179, *180*
Mullucks, Rhoda 230–1, *232–3*
Mullucks, Susan 230–1, *232–3*
Mumford, Lewis 67
Murrow, Ed 227–8

N

names 96

National Assistance Act (1948) 58
National Association for the Prevention of
  Tuberculosis 111
National Association for the Welfare of Children in
  Hospital 204
National Birth Control Association 155
National Birthday Trust Fund 83
National Childbirth Trust 134–7, 245
National Health Service (NHS) *36*, 68
  charities 126
  Family Planning Act (1967) 157
  foundation 24, 46, 75, 78, 80, 118, 135, 154, 244
  and GPs 80, 239–40
National Institute for Medical Research 111–12
National Insurance Act (1911) 78, 244
Neal, Patricia *209*
The New Yorker 67
News Chronicle 51
Newton, Sir Isaac 91
Nightingale, Florence 224
nitrous oxide 26
Noakes, Nurse 123
Noakes, Sgt 120, *211*
Northfield Military Hospital, Birmingham 172–3, 176
nutrition 74

O

Old-Age Pensions Act (1908) 78
Olympic Games (1948) 64–5
oral contraception 155, 245
Orwell, George 106
osteomalacia 75
Oxfam 126
oxytocin 53

P

Pages, Fidel 30
pain relief 25–31, 81, 84, 244, 245
Panum, Peter Ludvig 208
Pasteur, Louis 187, 244
pasteurisation 187, 220, 244
pathology 37
Pavlova, Anna 91
Peebles, Thomas 208
Peel, John 83
penicillin 47–53, *52*, 224, 244
penny licks 115, *115*
pethidine 30, 245
Peto, Sir Richard 227

Pfizer 51
phenothiazine drugs 171
phocomelia 230
Pickles, Wilfred 119
the pill 155, 245
Pinard, Adolph 91
'Pink Pills for Pale People' *110–11*
Pius XII, Pope 30
placenta, delivery of 53
Plath, Sylvia 135
Platt, Sir Robert 136
Platt Report (1959) 204, 245
pneumonia 48, 51, 220
polio 195–205, 208, 210, 245
Poor Law Commission (1906) 68, 69
poor relief 67
Poplar *24*, 31, 64
    abortions 150
    asbestosis in 228
    health standards in 96
    Lansbury Estate 65, *65, 66*, 67
    TB in 112, 114
Poplar Union Workhouse 67–8, *69*
post-mortems 37
post-natal clinics 155
post-natal depression 162, 164–5
post-puerperal psychosis 162, 164–5
poverty 67–8, 126
Powell, Enoch 64, *170*, 171
pre-eclampsia 37, 40, 41, 42
premature babies 41, 42, 90–3, *91*, 96
Presley, Elvis 203
prisoners of war 176, *176, 177*, 178
psychiatric problems 171, 220
Public Assistance Institutions 68
public health campaigns 80, 118
    birth control *156*
    polio *205*
    smoking *226*
    TB *108, 109*, 112
puerperal fever 53
pulmonary embolism 37

Q
quarantines 203
Queen Charlotte's Gas Air Analgesia Apparatus *31*

R
radiotherapy 228

Reed, Donna 210
relaxation 136
Rhodes, Cecil 67
rickets 70–5, *110–11*
Roberts, Douglas and Ruby 128–9
Robinson, Kenneth 240
Romans 150
Rothschild, Lord 113
Royal Commission on Medical Education 136
Royal Medical Society 42
Rubery Lunatic Asylum 176

S
Sabin, Albert 203
Saint, Pamela and George 164–5
St George's Hospital, Roehampton 238
Salk, Jonas 203, 204
salmonella 220
Salvarsan 187, 244
sanatoria 110, 112, 115
sanitation 214–21
Sargant, William 118
Saunders, Dame Cicely 126
scans, ultrasound 83
scarlet fever 194
School Medical Service 78
Scope 126
scurvy 74
Second World War (1939–45) 37, 126, 176, 225
    drug development during 30, 50, 53
    mental illness 170
Semmelweis, Dr Ignaz 54, 187, 244
sex education 154
Shelter 126
SIDS (sudden infant death syndrome) 32–7, 245
Sitwell, George 216
sleeping positions, babies 35, 37
smallpox 184–5, 244, 245
Smart, Dolly 40
Smellie, William 84, 88
smoking 225–8, *226*
Snoddy, Alice and Albert 67
Society for the Prevention of Cruelty to Pregnant
    Women 136
spastics 119, 126
The Spastics Society 119, *119*, 120
spina bifida 128–9
Spock, Dr Benjamin 35
Steel, David 152, 245

sterilising feeding equipment 96
stillbirth 90, 98–9, 123
stirrups 90
Stoeckel, Walter 30
Stopes, Marie *153*, 154–5, *155*, 157
Streptococcus pnuemoniae 51
streptomycin 113
Strongyloides stercoralis 176, 178–9
sudden infant death syndrome (SIDS) 32–7, 245
sulphonamides 53, 90, 244
The Sunday Times 235, *236*, 238
symphysiotomy 88, 90
syphilis 187, 244

T

thalidomide 230–8, *234*, *235*, *236*
Thalidomide Society 238
Thatcher, Margaret 83
toxaemia 37, 40
tracheotomy 189–90, 194
Trilene 25, *25*, 26
tuberculin 109
tuberculosis (TB) 102–15, 142, 187, 244
Turner, Angela 143, *158–9*, 160, 161
Turner, Joe 52
Turner, Marianne 18, 20, 196
Turner, Shelagh (Sister Bernadette) 31, 34, *95*, *138*, 196, 207
  and Angela 143, *158–9*
  and Dr Turner 139–45, 149
  dysentery 216, 219
  Mave Carter's twins 18, 20, 138
  Susan Mullucks 230
  TB 102, 104, 113, 142
Turner, Timothy 62, 140, 148–9
  death of mother 20, 28, 140, 142
  polio 142–3, *192–3*, 196–201
Twain, Mark 91
twins 18–21, 83
typhoid 220, 221, 222–5

U

ultrasound scans 83
unmarried mothers 30, 150, 151, 152
uterine bleeding 53

V

vaccinations 184–6, 188, 189
  BCG vaccination *107*, 109–10, 115, 244
  diphtheria 244
  measles 208, *208*, 209–10, 245
  polio 198, 203–4, *203*, 205, 245
  smallpox 184–5, 244
  typhoid 224
Vera Drake 153, 154
Vickers, Merle and Billy 130–1
Victoria, Queen 25, 88, 194, 224
Vinall, Dorothy *85*
vitamins 74–5

W

Wakefield, Andrew 210
Waksman, Selman 113
Walker-Smith, Derek 203
war neurosis 172–3, 176
Ward, Mrs 87
Willington, Sally 136
Wilson, G. S. 112–13
Wimbish, Colette 92–3, *94–5*
Winifred, Sister *138*
wise women 78
workhouses 58, 62, 67–9
World Health Assembly 184
World Health Organization 210, 239, 245
Worth, Jennifer 153–4, 155
Wright, Almroth 50, 224

X

X-ray machines 102, 104, 109, 113, 244

Y

Yokohama *176*
Yorkshire Post 229
Your Life in Their Hands 118

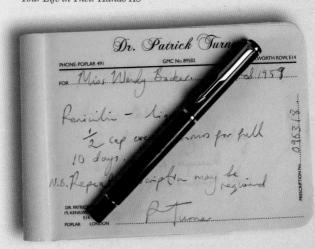

PICTURE CREDITS

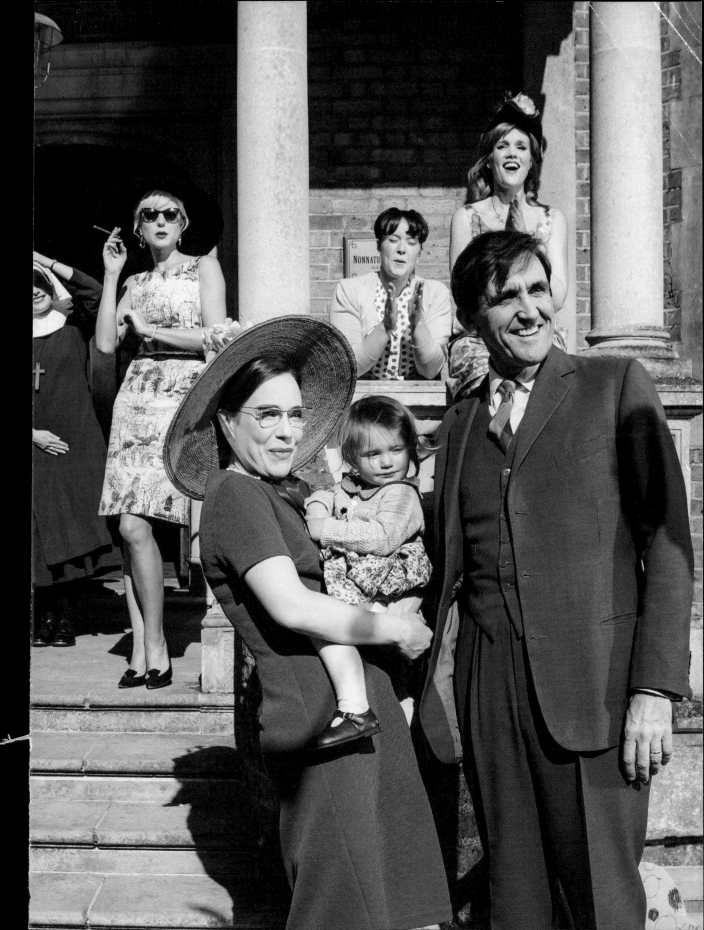

ACKNOWLEDGEMENTS

My thanks to the matchless and inspirational Dame Pippa Harris and everybody at Neal Street Productions for their brilliant creativity and vision; to Iain MacGregor and everybody at Simon and Schuster for their endless skill, patience and support in writing this book; and to the wonderful Karen Farrington for helping to bring it all to the page.

Thanks to the lovely Annie Tricklebank and all the production team on *Call the Midwife*, for their talent in making a globally successful drama series seem so easy to achieve; to my fellow actors on *Call the Midwife*, without whom this book could simply never have been written - Helen George, Jenny Agutter, Judy Parfitt, Pam Ferris, Miranda Hart, Emerald Fennell, Charlotte Ritchie, Jessica Raine, Bryony Hannah, Cliff Parisi, Linda Bassett, Jack Ashton, Victoria Yeates, Kate Lamb, Ben Caplan, and my brilliant screen son Max Macmillan. I'd especially like to thank my screen wife Laura Main, whose lucid and moving portrayal provides so much of the emotional and moral context to Patrick's character.

Deepest thanks to my real-life son Dominic: for his wit, his warmth, and the enduring gift of fatherhood. Lastly, all thanks to my dear companion Heidi Thomas - creator of the *Call the Midwife* series and my wife of twenty five years. For her unequalled skill in bringing to life the character of Doctor Turner and the world he inhabits; for her genius in communicating the human compassion that informs all good drama and all good medicine; and for the endless love and humour that lights my life.